CABI CONCISE

LEISURE IN ACTION

Since *leisure* is no longer identified as something that is important in social, cultural, political and economic spheres, its essentiality in all our lives is increasingly overlooked. For many people, the use of the word 'leisure' is merely regarded as something that is archaic, unfashionable or done by people who are uninteresting and work-shy. By contrast, sport has managed to maintain its importance, especially in policy-making circles, because it is good for the economy and a powerful platform for expressing national sentiment. As for physical activity, it has found a role to play in health policy, where it is promoted as a solution to mental health disorders and obesity. Leisure, meanwhile, has been reduced to an adjunct to work – something lacking in novelty that is done to rest and recuperate before the next working day begins.

As a critical response, this series challenges the idea that leisure is redundant in the 21st century. It follows that the series should be viewed as a forum for showing how the activities we can place under the heading 'leisure' are varied and diverse in the contemporary world, and that it is these activities that make human beings and human culture.

The aim of this series is first and foremost to explore the ever-changing landscape of leisure which has transformed significantly in the last 30 years or so, with a shift in focus from 'big' leisure interests to activities that are less bounded and infinitely more imaginative and diverse. Of particular interest are leisure spaces, sites for leisure activities and things that are part of leisure that too easily go unnoticed.

As well as examining current trends in individual and collective leisure activities, the series is a forum for succinct and highly readable research that examines our contemporary world of leisure through the lens of real-world experience. The focus is on mapping current developments and promoting discussion and critical analysis about the lived significance of leisure as a means of engaging with the challenges and opportunities of human existence. To encourage and promote methodological innovation the series encourages the use of narrative inquiry, and it places strong emphasis on the use of empirical evidence to make meaning from experiences. Targeting academics who prefer to frame their leisure worlds using rich detail, the series is about using bodies-in-action to conduct research that is not only intimate, intuitive and empathetic but also challenges conventional interpretations of leisure.

Kevin Bingham
KBingham@lincoln.ac.uk

Dedication

For Jenny. My wife, my confidante, my love.

The Book of Walking Dangerously: Notes from a Theatre of Memory

Kevin P. Bingham

University of Lincoln, UK

CABI

CABI is a trading name of CAB International

CABI
Nosworthy Way
Wallingford
Oxfordshire OX10 8DE
UK

CABI
200 Portland Street
Boston
MA 02114
USA

Tel: +44 (0)1491 832111
E-mail: info@cabi.org
Website: www.cabi.org

T: +1 (617)682-9015
E-mail: cabi-nao@cabi.org

The views expressed in this publication are those of the author(s) and do not necessarily represent those of, and should not be attributed to, CAB International (CABI). Any images, figures and tables not otherwise attributed are the author(s)' own. References to internet websites (URLs) were accurate at the time of writing.

CAB International and, where different, the copyright owner shall not be liable for technical or other errors or omissions contained herein. The information is supplied without obligation and on the understanding that any person who acts upon it, or otherwise changes their position in reliance thereon, does so entirely at their own risk. Information supplied is neither intended nor implied to be a substitute for professional advice. The reader/user accepts all risks and responsibility for losses, damages, costs and other consequences resulting directly or indirectly from using this information.

CABI's Terms and Conditions, including its full disclaimer, may be found at https://www.cabidigitallibrary.org/terms-and-conditions.

A catalogue record for this book is available from the British Library, London, UK.

ISBN-13: 9781836993247 (hardback)
 9781836993254 (paperback)
 9781836993261 (ePDF)
 9781836993278 (ePub)

DOI: 10.1079/9781836993278.0000

Commissioning Editor: Rebecca Stubbs
Editorial Assistant: Theresa Regueira
Production Editor: Rosie Hayden

Typeset by Exeter Premedia Services Pvt Ltd, Chennai, India
Printed and bound in the UK by CPI Group (UK) Ltd, Croydon, CR0 4YY

Contents

Foreword

One of the most interesting developments in leisure studies over the last twenty-odd years has been the fragmentation of general knowledge and awareness into specific interest. Nowhere is this trend more apparent than in the study of those free-time activities concerned with, as says A. C. Grayling, 'cultivating life's amenities'. If the present volume is anything to go by, there will be no better test-bed than this new CABI book series *Leisure in Action* for examining what leisure teaches us about this 'cultivating' and how it enables us to find our own free and liberated relation to the world.

Since the focus of the series is on leisure, its subject matter is inherently *interdisciplinary*. In this first volume, written by the Editor, Kevin Bingham, the boundaries between sociology, philosophy, cultural geography and psychology become blurred. However, the intellectual power of its indisciplinary thesis derives in no small part from its author's disregard of more conventional ways of exploring walking as a leisure activity, made possible by the extraordinary compass of his scholarship. Bingham has one of the most daring outlooks of scholars interested in understanding the dynamics of everyday leisure, publishing the two research monographs An *Ethnography of Urban Exploration: Unpacking Heterotopic Social Space* (Palgrave MacMillan, 2020) and *Exploring the Natural Underground: A New Sociology of Caving* (Routledge, 2023). In the present volume he offers his readers a paralogy of walking dangerously, which shows us that scholarly inquiry and leisure are not only synonymous, but just like other forms of human existence and creation, are nothing if not risky business – after all, despite our best intentions, things often go wrong. The main premise of its thesis is that we should embrace this risk and see it as something anarchic that properly belongs to all leisure worthy of the name.

As with all adventure stories, the big picture is here, but so is the spirited turn of phrase, a keen eye for the telling detail, and a gift for applying complex philosophical insights. Walking off the beaten track, Bingham takes his readers on a journey from South Yorkshire to the North Yorkshire Moors, to the Lake District National Park, across the English Channel to walk an abandoned section of the Maginot Line in north-eastern France, through the years of his doctoral studies in New Zealand, to his return to England and the Peak District near his home near Sheffield. Taken together, these walks provide us with a tantalizing picture of the mixture of necessary and precipitating conditions of risky leisure which say yes to the fear and absurdity of the primal elements, and by so doing help us to come to grips with ourselves and what Emmanuel Levinas called the 'beautiful risk' of creation and re-creation.

Readers who think they know everything about walking, think again. Bingham's gripping narrative shows how its too often overlooked hazards enjoin us all to extend ourselves as individuals, insisting that the risks they bring, open up new possibilities and expectations. Set against the backdrops of some of the most fearsome milieux nature can offer, the impact this book has on its readers will stay long after the final page.

This is the work of a dedicated scholar, and every page is energized by his intelligence and imagination. Prepare for an experience of walking unlike any other you've ever encountered before.

Tony Blackshaw
Emeritus Professor of Leisure Studies and Sociology, Sheffield Hallam University

References

Grayling, A.C. (2000) 'The last word on... Leisure. The Guardian. [Online]. Retrieved from: https://www.theguardian.com/books/2000/feb/05/books.guardianreview7

Levinas, E., cited in Gert J.J. Biesta (2016) *The Beautiful Risk of Education*. London and New York: Routledge.

Acknowledgements

To the boys around the fire, when the night is ours to laugh and let wild memories free. To a little girl with a big imagination, full of life and wonder. To a selfless wife and best friend. And, to a Commissioning Editor who settled on walking dangerously. To each of you, I give my thanks.

Drafting a Theatre of Memory for Paralogical Concerns

1

1.1 Introduction

Helvellyn Scramble. Photo © K.P. Bingham

Surrounded by mist and doused in drizzle, I set out to traverse the crest of Striding Edge, a route that is thought to be one of the deadliest of the Lakeland Fells because valleys fall away at either side of the narrow ridgeway. Famously, the ridge is described by Alfred Wainwright (1955/2009) as 'all bare rock, a succession of jagged fangs ending in a black tower'. From the famous Gap in the Wall bad weather had drifted in; thick, ethereal fog that snagged and snared at every visible crag without mercy. Enrobing me, I became blind and the landscape perfectly silent. Red Tarn which had been visible in the basin below moments earlier, whose water's edge had been dotted with tents, was suddenly swallowed and banished into nothingness. Tentatively, I ventured on.

Soon I found myself scrambling up the rocks of Wainwright's intimidating black tower, aiming to reach a trail stretching along the infamous ridge with near-vertical precipices on either side. As I reached the head of the barbican the fog parted momentarily, allowing me to steal a glimpse of the ridge of fangs. Ahead, an organic crenelated wall was revealed, a shattered barricade of crag and scree curving upwards towards the smooth plateau of the mountain's summit. Unable to enjoy the view for long, the weather moved in again. Once more I found myself alone.

Filled with anticipation, fearing I might unwittingly step off the ridgeway and tumble into the invisible abyss, I edged my way along the spine of Striding Edge. Although I knew a safer bypass footpath ran somewhere below on the right, I opted to clamber the naked rock head on. Clambering the precipice while enveloped in heavy fog brought on mild symptoms of vertigo, a sudden feeling of there being a loss of equilibrium between body and earth that could easily have been mistaken for dizziness. The feeling made me unstable and less confident in my ability to walk. Accompanying the vertigo was the terrifying and unshakable sense that something bad was about to happen.

As I neared the summit of Helvellyn I faced one final ascent, a face of rock streaming with water. By this point, the fog had thinned. Darts of rain had managed to break through, dispersing the otherworldly veil to allow through a steadier stream of fatter droplets. With my head bowed against the driving rain, I continued until I was at long last spat onto the firmer ground of the plateau. With my back turned against the razor-sharp edge, I gathered my bearings and headed for the memorial commemorating Charles Gough, an artist of the early Romantic movement who perished tackling the very same route as he was making his way to the small village of Grasmere.

My ascent of Helvellyn marked the starting point of a new writing project. As I reached the head of Wainwright's black tower, the fog parted momentarily to reveal an organic crenelated wall. As I gazed out across Striding Edge, a weather-beaten arête that twists upwards towards a flat-topped summit, I wondered whether there was something original to be said about *walking*. Finally, after a period of restlessness following the completion of a book about caving, it seemed I had a new idea to grapple with. In that moment, I had plans to walk as far as my legs could take me in search of wild and potentially hazardous experiences.

In truth, it was not Helvellyn alone that inspired me. At the time I was working my way through a collection of travelogues, those written by Lauire Lee (1969/2014), Patrick Leigh Fermor (1977/2005) and Bruce Chatwin (1988), and what appealed to me is that each one was written with appreciation for honesty and intimacy. I might argue that each one has verisimilitude and artistic flair, characteristics that are fading from travelogues of the day which are more popularly called online travel blogs. With the summer newly beginning, I estimated I had just enough time to follow in Lee's footsteps and head to mainland Spain by way of foot. Intending to stick close to Grantham,

Peterborough, Cambridge and London initially, I set Madrid as my end point. My aim, I decided, was to embark on a journey filled with the uncertainty of adventure, possibilities for discovering new ideas and of course the usual obstacles and instances of despair that accompany any person on a long trip away from home.

It did not take long at all, however, for reality to set in. With commitments to family and work, I had to accept that the project was unrealistic. Returning my attention to the drawing board, I had a rethink. I eventually settled on the idea that I perhaps already had plenty of material for a new book in the form of memories and piles of unused notes from years of hiking, urban exploring and caving. This material, I pondered, could still take my readers on a journey that would not be too far removed from my original idea. Instead of travelling to Spain though, we would travel together as far as New Zealand.

1.2   Choosing How to Walk

Before I could start writing, an important decision had to be made. Since there are many ways of walking, I had to decide how exactly I was going to walk. I had to think, that is, about the myriad types of strolling, striding and perambulating that have been experimented with before in various theoretical and methodological ways. To begin with, I wondered whether a useful starting point might be the perennial figure of the flâneur.

Although the origins of the term *flâneur* are unknown, records from as early the 1630s indicate it derives from the Norman verb 'flanner' ("to waste" or "to laze") and the ancient Scandinavian word 'flana' ("to run here and there"). The word's vague etymology notwithstanding, the term has been used widely in more recent literary writings to refer to a portrait of the modern European man who is not only a product of modern European society but the prototype of the present-day consumer. From the early nineteenth century then the flâneur has been viewed as classically bourgeois. Unaffected by routines and responsibilities associated with everyday life, the flâneur was seen instead to be driven by an insatiable curiosity for the varied and constantly changing aesthetics of the spectacle of the city. Due to his higher status, the flâneur stood out as an individual with freedom of movement and time to idly interpret the landscape of the city. Eventually, the flâneur became better known as the figure of Paris. Impeccably dressed and with knowledge of the fashions and manners of refined Parisian society, this was a figure that could remain relaxed and tranquil while roaming without rhyme or reason.

What appealed to me about the flâneur is that he not only represents the quintessential man of leisure but accentuates the importance of getting lost. I also liked the suggestion, as Walter Benjamin (1968) states, that the flâneur is a threatened species whom history is about to overtake. What Benjamin was acknowledging is that the haunt of the flâneur, the old arcades with their sophisticated façades, luxury shops and pleasant cafés, was already long past its heyday when he was writing. All the flâneur can do, therefore, is pore over modernity's remains to prompt recollections of times gone by. Recognising the significance of the flâneur's need for leisure, solitude and the past, I felt there was perhaps a connection to my idea of walking. The immediate problem I had, however, were I to become a flâneur, is that too much emphasis is given to detachment and being able to drift as an observer rather than an engager of the environment. What I wanted was involvement in the action, so the metaphor did not quite fit the bill.

Looking beyond flâneurism, I began to think about the broader practice of psychogeography which generally involves walking. Although many psychogeographers idolise the flâneur, my understanding is that there is more to psychogeography because there are a variety of traditions. Furthermore, psychogeography typically involves active exploration as opposed to passive and detached motion.

The origins of the term psychogeography can be traced back to Guy Debord (1955) and the Lettrist Group (a group of radical theorists and artists) in 1950s Paris. The original definition invented by Debord describes it as a colliding point between psychology and geography and 'the study of the specific effects of the geographical environment, consciously organised or not, on the emotions and behaviour of individuals'. Part of Debord's treatise was his theory of the dérive ("drifting") which is the technique of dropping usual motives for action and movement to transiently pass through different ambiences in playful and constructive ways. Under the direction of Debord, psychogeography became a popularly used tool, first for aesthetic purposes but later political motives.

Today, as Merlin Coverley (2006) points out, many psychogeographers have managed to escape the oppressive orthodoxy of Debord's dogma. While psychogeography still involves walking on foot, it has been used extensively as a means of searching for myriad ways of experiencing urban environments. What unites most psychogeographers is that they seek to overcome the drab monotony of everyday surroundings. Using playful activities, provocation and trickery, the layouts of urban labyrinths are reworked and reimagined to discover new insights about the lives of cities. This is psychogeography as intensely personal mythology, a collection of ideas that try to push the boundaries of creativity and imagination. The other side is one of protest and opposition. In cities that are becoming more hostile to pedestrians, psychogeography serves as a method of subversion since walking conflicts perfectly with the spirit of modern cities and their promotion of swift circulation. Writing from a car-choked Paris, Jean-Christophe Bailly (1992) expounds on this idea with his suggestion that the social and imaginative function of cities 'is under threat from the tyranny of bad architecture, soulless planning and indifference to the basic unit of urban language, the street, and the "ruissellement de paroles" (stream of words), the endless stories, which animate it'. Should walking cease, Bailly warns, the stories that keep cities alive will become unread or even unreadable.

After some time in the perusal of literature, I decided in the end that psychogeography was not for me. Nuances were emerging and they complicated matters. First, there was the problem that psychogeographic experiments are an urban affair as they look to disrupt and challenge official representations of cities. Since I wanted to include stories involving caving and rural hiking in the book, some of my content would be completely unrelated to urban environments. Second, as Iain Sinclair (see: Kelso, 2016) pointed out in a 2016 interview – despite having exploited the practice for years as a way of psychoanalysing the psychosis of London – psychogeography has outlived its usefulness and become a brand. The fact everyone is doing it serves as a reminder that everything, even the radical, is appropriable and consumable by the general public. This was a problem because I still wanted to write something outside the limits of convention to signal that there can be different logic to walking.

With psychogeography set to one side, my attention turned to other literature that deals with walking as method or methodology. To start with I came across Maggie O'Neill and Brian Roberts's (2020) method of 'the walking interview as a biographical method'. As a form of ethnography, this methodological approach involves carrying out interviews on the move to construct a complete impression of an individual's life and experience. Following the argument that people have complex social and environmental relations and changing sensual, cognitive and relational feelings, the method enables researchers to meet people within their natural surroundings and take part in their routine activities. In short, the walking interview enables researchers to investigate individuals as socially located but also mobile in time, space and mental life, and it can show how people consciously respond to their social and natural environments through the creation of embodied reflections and evaluations.

Before I went any further with ethnographic walking biographies, however, I debated whether the book I had in mind might paint a deeper, richer and altogether fuller evocation of walking dangerously if I used myself as the central and only character. Dissatisfied with the perceived need for many ethnographers to model themselves after scientists, factfinders or detectives of the field, I settled on the idea of wanting to shift my focus from an act of chronicling events to one of diaristic gesture. Understanding the significance of my own body as a medium for performance, I wondered whether I might instigate an unrestrained investigation, one capable of reshaping and reimagining the world, act by act, object by object, with something so simple as walking. Available to me as content, I thought, were my own personal memories of events, encounters, actions and experiences. Rather than rely on others who might struggle to communicate or make sense of their experiences, or leave room on my behalf for potential misinterpretation, I felt that my own stories could be elicited more vividly and with greater emotion.

The idea for some kind of travelogue came next. Knowing from the start it would be impossible to embark on a walk for any long period of time, I probed the literature for examples of other sorts of travelogue. According to the original definition, the term is a portmanteau of the words 'travel' and 'monologue', and it is taken to mean the first-person narration of experiences of travelling. Usually, they are written in the style of a memoir rather than a guidebook and throughout history their rich detail has helped readers travel to far-flung lands and regions without ever having to leave the comfort of their own armchairs. Whereas early accounts of travel tended to document objective facts in an impersonal style, from the late seventeenth century writings became more personal and subjective to capture the thoughts, feelings and introspection of an author.

Recently, the focus of some travelogue methodologies has shifted to palimpsestic journeying in the form of 'microtravel' or 'micro adventuring'. The phenomenon of *microtravel*, as described by Charles Forsdick, Zoë Kinsley and Kate Walchester (2024), gained increased recognition following the COVID-19 pandemic which imposed immobility and confinement across much of the everyday world. The general idea is that restriction can lead to a mode of travelling associated with slowing down and perceiving places differently. Walking is said to exemplify the impact of deceleration as it ensures close contact with the field of travel and therefore activates multisensory forms of engagement. The phenomenon of the micro or backyard adventure made popular by Alastair Humphreys (2014) and Beau Miles (2021) is about being intimate with everyday places. Although the act of walking is not absolutely essential in a microadventure since it can take many forms (a four-day commute to work via kayak in Miles's case), it facilitates the simplest, easiest to organise and most affordable kind of adventure.

A micro travelogue methodology seemed almost perfect, and I came very close to running with it, but I had a niggling concern that was difficult to shift. My concern was with the problematic legacy of travel literature since travelogues from the nineteenth century are typically predicated on colonial superiority and the internalised attitude of ethnic or cultural inferiority. Wanting, therefore, to not only avoid association with narratives that perpetuate hegemonic masculinity, social injustice and racism but also produce something involving reflexivity and close inspection of my sense of self, I began to wonder whether I could devise my own kind of walking. This could be a form of walking, I thought, with its own distinctive elements, and new rules concerning its structure and content.

1.3   Experimenting with Method to Walk Dangerously

Now I have provided an overview of various ways of walking, I want to be clear about the exact focus of this book. My overarching aim is not to provide a walking guide or a history of walking. Neither is it to explore the functional or therapeutic nature of walking, idolise the flâneur, or engage in the practice of psychogeography. Scholars and travel writers have done all of this, and many have done it well. Very simply, the kind of walking that interested me from the start would involve actions and events I knew would bring me closer to possibilities of enduring something unwelcome and unpleasant, or suffering, harm and injury. These are objectionable things I would be less likely to experience if I were to engage in walking as a normal, everyday pursuit. What I wanted to do is *walk dangerously*.

Before I address the dangerous component a little more and explain its significance, I want to be clear that walking in my mind is more than being able to move at a regular pace by lifting and setting each foot down in turn. To walk might be to step, saunter, clump, march, stride, trudge, trample, ramble, traverse, roam, clamber, stagger, falter or scramble. I am conscious as well that it can be pleasurable or utilitarian but also unpleasant and seemingly meaningless. And, although we do it routinely under familiar conditions, often engaging in little to no thought, it can be an embodied physical and mental experience that ignites the senses in all kinds of strange and unfamiliar environments.

With my definition of walking outlined, the interpretation in this book is that walking dangerously is about introspection – the act of looking inward and exploring new thoughts and feelings when opportunities arise. My suggestion is not that new thoughts and feelings have to be pleasurable and shaped by sources of ecstasy and freedom, it is that people can still have fulfilling leisure lives if they are willing to deal, for a short while at least, with disagreeableness. Too often, or so my argument in this book goes, people are eager to ignore their dangerous spirit for fear of encountering displeasure, so my proposition is that we should sometimes choose to embrace it. What this book does therefore, intimately, intuitively and empathetically, is deal with what I am tempted to call the delicate art of displeasure and the disagreeable. My way of doing exactly this, on the back of having walked dangerously for a number of years, has been to unfold a *paralogy*.

Borrowing the term from the field of biology, Jean-François Lyotard (1984) introduces the idea of paralogy in his treatise *The Postmodern Condition*. In his own formulation, he alludes to a version of antilogic closely related to Derridean deconstruction. First and foremost, paralogy is a sociology and a method that might also be described as a response to a problem in present-day society. More specifically, it is a response to the speculation that the metanarratives of modernity have failed. Secondly, as Lyotard explains, it is about undermining from within. It is about replacing a familiar narrative with a different one within a dominant language game. The problem with familiar narratives is that they obey rules and convention as they involve epistemological frameworks and are contaminated by 'the rational'. A paralogy, however, is a way of deconstructing regimes of truth and resisting their power for totality.

In the case of this book, paralogy is celebrated as a means of recognising there can be different logic to life that most sociologists, flâneurs and psychogeographers ignore or perhaps do not understand. Ultimately, my aim with this book is to force a rethinking, a destabilising of existing rules, that is not geared toward reproductivity of pleasure and enjoyment or what is generally accepted as 'normal' academic study. To better explain what I mean, I want to interject with an imaginary universe presented by Jorge Luis Borges (1940/1998). The story is a useful example of a paralogical world Lyotard is advocating.

> At first it was believed that Tlön was a mere chaos, an irresponsible license of the imagination; now it is known that it is a cosmos and that the intimate laws which govern it have been formulated, at least provisionally... Every mental state

is irreducible: the mere fact of naming it implies a falsification. From which it can be deduced that there are no sciences on Tlön, not even reasoning. The paradoxical truth is that they do exist, and in almost unaccountable number... The metaphysicians of Tlön do not seek the truth or even for verisimilitude, but rather for the astounding. They judge that metaphysics is a branch of fantastic literature. They know that a system is nothing more than subordination of all aspects of the universe to any one such aspect. Even the phrase "all aspects" is rejectable, for it supposes the impossible addition of the present and of all past moments.

What Borges's universe mirrors, if we pay attention, is a child's world. There is something playful and game-like to it as fact and fiction become blurred and magically entwined. What is being sought by Borges, just as a child's actions and language games illustrate, is a kind of *amazement*. The problem with this type of thinking, however, is that it is typically abandoned in favour of incredulity and subordination. As Ludwig Wittgenstein (1921/1998) explains, a characteristic phenomenon of our world is that people share an eagerness to impose rational thought and forcibly unite objects by making logical connections. Consequently, curiosity and amazement are too easily cast aside and forgotten.

In this book, my way of reinvigorating sensitivities to differences and toleration of the incommensurable is to capture, intimately, intuitively and empathetically, the *amazement* of *displeasure* and the *disagreeable*. The starting point is my willingness to listen to Borges and his invitation to free ourselves to speculate about alternative versions of experiences. My claim is that striving for a paralogy is one way of doing this. The quest for paralogy is about celebrating heterogeneity and diversity, and cultivating a spirit of imagination, wonder and astonishment. It is also about celebrating the ill-defined, the unknowable and the unpresentable. What I set out to do, then, as I traverse steep arêtes in the fog, slip through wreckage and broken mortar, and venture deep inside the enigmatic Kingdom of the Dark is reveal the suppressible or ignored elements of walking that exist within its logical constructs. On the back of this, it is my intention that I will show how contradictions and aporias are invaluable if we are to make better sense of assorted leisure worlds.

The vision for what follows starts with Friedrich Nietzsche's (1882/2001) assertion that ideas do not belong merely among books. As he puts it, 'it is our habit to think outdoors – walking, leaping, climbing, dancing, preferably on lonely mountains or near the sea where even the trails become thoughtful'. His point is that many books are produced from readings of earlier texts which causes them to secrete stale odours. For Nietzsche, these are grey books spilling with citations, quotations, footnotes, academic jargon and boundless refutations, all belonging to the dark aisles of stuffy libraries. There are other books, however, that release a livelier air – the freshness of a crisp morning, the sting of icy ocean wind, or the intoxicating, resinous scent of pine forest. These are the kind of books, born of human action, that breathe. In a nutshell then, what I have sought to produce is an immersive first-hand account that is scrupulous in capturing the amazement of displeasure and the disagreeable.

Drawing inspiration from those ethnographers who are accomplished practitioners of hermeneutic sociology, such as Henning Bech (1997) with his phenomenological study *When Men Meet* and George Orwell (1933/2013) with *Down and Out in Paris and London*, this book is intimate in the way it tells readers what it feels like to walk dangerously. As I have described elsewhere in monographs about urban exploration and caving, having originally borrowed the idea from Tony Blackshaw (2003), this approach involves being a little like Lewis Carroll's Alice who after tumbling down the rabbit hole discovers she has entered an entirely new world. It is, as Bech (1997) would say, a way of snuggling up to the actual reality of an existing discourse. As this style of writing exposes the pure magic and intimacy of existence, my intention is that readers will encounter enough vividity and intensity they will feel invited to be part of it.

1.4   A Theatre of Memory

Earlier I noted that starting a new project from scratch would have been an unrealistic undertaking because, at the present time, family and work commitments are my priority. This meant I was faced with an immediate dilemma in that I had a topic but seemingly nothing to write about and no content to bring to life. After much deliberation it was finally Raphael Samuel's (1994) book, *Theatres of Memory*, that gave me an idea for an alternative approach. As it would turn out, this unorthodox tactic would tie nicely with my celebration of paralogy and the claim that a different logic is needed if walking dangerously is to be better understood and appreciated.

Before outlining my approach, I first want to explain that Samuel, as a Marxist historian, sought to disrupt the academic hierarchy of historical knowledge by valuing public memory as an essential aspect of historical understanding. As he viewed things, history is not a fixed, objective record but something that is dynamic and contested as it is created and recreated in everyday life. For ordinary people, he argues, a wide range of cultural forms such as family stories, monuments, museums and reenactments are used to shape historical narratives and make sense of the past. His central idea, then, is that 'theatres of memory' are important. They are subjective spaces where understandings of the past are performed, debated and negotiated outside of formal institutions.

Inspired by Samuel, my attention turned to the idea that memory can be used as method. As an active participant I could engage with, and even create, representations of the past. Moreover, I could include my own 'unofficial knowledge' of the past. My intention, I decided, was to remain true to the voices of my past and at the same time maintain some of the violence of abstraction. What I mean by this is that I wanted to write a book that is not only self-consciously authentic and sincere but also captures the natural chaos and fallibility of human recollection. With passions driving it, curious paradoxes lurking in the undergrowth and loose ends left untied, this is a book that serves to seduce, mesmerise and confound. It proffers tantalising glimpses of a world of my own creation in a way that invites readers to come along on a journey that exists somewhere between the real, the reconstructed and the phantastic.

Although the use of memory as method has to the best of my knowledge not been widely used in studies of walking, it is a tried and tested method that goes as far back as Aristotle and Cicero. For example, philosophers have long used mnemonic systems – techniques to help improve the recollection of important information – to arrange memories in physical locations. Often something architectural has been relied on as a mnemonic device such as a palace or theatre. The structure might consist of a series of rooms or levels, each representing items of knowledge a person may at some point wish to retrieve and use.

The origins of the method notwithstanding, while planning the book I still felt there was an underlying problem with my idea. What I was proposing was not quite enough. It did not seem adequate to merely state that 'unofficial knowledge' of the past would be used as a method since critics would no doubt argue it lacks depth and substance. What I want to argue, therefore, is that there are three important elements to consider when dealing with remembered content. The elements include *performance, mediation* and *spatiality*. This is an idea I pieced together from Liedeke Plate and Anneke Smelik's (2013) volume on *Performing Memory in Art and Popular Culture*.

Firstly, performance should be understood as embodied behaviour and the privileging of praxis over product and body over speech. Crucially, it is a way of knowing that can only be obtained if a person has breathed in the here and now of a live event. To draw memories from this kind of knowledge is to carefully exploit habitual memory that has, to an extent, become sedimented in the body. Performance memory is also theatrical and lively which gives it both a radical edge and a sense of realness *par excellence*. In a nutshell, only the excitement and momentum of an original event is powerful enough to bring back a past capable of disrupting the present.

Secondly, it must be accepted that memory does not function alone inside an impregnable vacuum. As it is widely acknowledged, people are shaped by social, generational and cultural contexts which means memories cannot help but be heavily influenced by things such as digitalisation and medial communication and technology. In short, memory is increasingly mediated in the twenty-first century. A key consequence is that technologies not only play a key role in how people perceive events but also in the whole process of remembering. The internet, for example, with its inestimable digital myths, has been successful in deindividualising and depersonalising memory and in blurring the boundaries between the real and unreal.

Finally, it is generally agreed that memories must be stored somewhere and this is where spatial metaphors have traditionally been used. Popular spatial metaphors, up until the 1980s at least, were images of place (rooms, houses, theatres, palaces etc.) and scholars have viewed memory as something that is recoverable since it is permanently stored in the mind. Such a view is too static for me. My interpretation of memory is more dynamic because memories, as I see them, are conceived as reconstructions rather than reproductions and therefore exist as rhizomatic networks involving multidirectionality. As Gilles Deleuze and Félix Guattari (1987) explain, rhizomes spread in all kinds of directions to create a chaotic network where one point might be connected to any other point. As I reflected on Samuel's (1994) argument that the visual should be taken more seriously as a mode of knowledge and his suggestion that photographs are a vital part of 'unofficial knowledge', I decided photographs would be a way of dealing with spatiality.

My way of ensuring there was appropriate fitness between memory and events that really occurred was to give due attention to the three elements outlined above. Hence, the contents of the book only consists of lived, first-hand experiences. What I wanted to offer readers is an accumulation in my mind of everything I have seen, heard, touched, smelt and even tasted whilst walking dangerously. As for the impact of existing social, generational and cultural contexts, attention has been given to sociological hermeneutics. The practice of sociological hermeneutics, as Zygmunt Bauman (1992) explains, involves having awareness and comprehension of the bigger factors that bear down on our lives so I have been mindful throughout this book of the surface phenomena that cannot help but be part of our leisure worlds and the societies in which we live. As for something spatial, I made use of photographs to help recollect and arrange relevant memorial content. The spatial information contained within a photograph which we perceive as depth and dimension may well be fluid and indefinite, but it allows a viewer to re-experience moments in time.

For some people, a photograph album is a means of bringing memories tumbling back into the present. For me, my loft served the purpose because hundreds of framed photographs of abandoned places, cave chambers and natural landscapes adorn the walls. The 'gallery' as I am tempted to call it has been an essential part of the process of writing this book since it has allowed me to buttress memories of my adventures with visual impetuses and tokens of lived experience. The gallery has also been useful in the way it regularly transforms. Although the images are fixed and rarely changed, in my mind the display never remains the same for too long since it succeeds in stimulating my imagination. As John Berger (2008) explains, every image embodies a different way of seeing. Seeing can remind us of why we originally took a photograph, why we decided to capture one specific moment, but it can also conjure up things that are missing. As I gaze into the depths of my pictures, I can reflect on everything I am prevented from seeing and how everything visual has the power to entice different gazes and interpretations. Sometimes, I find that the photographs on display can even be replaced by other pictures that are stored away or in fact were never taken.

1.5   An Outline of the Book

What follows in the remainder of the book resembles travel writing. But rather than describe each journey in full, I leave it up to the reader to do some of the work. A walk of any kind should express freedom and space and I wanted to impress this upon the reader's imagination, so what I ask of my readers is that they interpret the ambiguous and imagine the unseen. Through their lack of emphasis, the formal and quantifiable aspects of walking – duration, measurement, geometry – should be temporarily disregarded in this book. Instead, emphasis sits with the abstractions of language in which a walk can be described. Locations, too, even if they seem familiar to the reader, should be difficult to place on any real map because they are places of reconstruction before they are determinable. In the true sense of the idea that history is a living process that is continually reinterpreted and reevaluated, this book consists of notes from a theatre of memory.

Following a style similar in some ways to Italo Calvino's (1997) *Invisible Cities*, a travelogue of anti-structure that describes fifty-five fictitious cities, the book sets out to unpack seven disparate and unrelated walks conjured by imagination and memory. Each episode is intentionally poetic and involves careful mediations on the nature of my own experience. The point of each chapter is to present the constant activity of the human mind while it is busy desiring, dreaming and escaping, and it does so, not unlike Calvino's character Marco Polo who never really leaves his hometown of Venice, without ever leaving the reassuring cosiness of my loft. Naturally, not everything in this text is magical and enchanting. Most of it, as explained earlier in the chapter, addresses displeasure and the disagreeable. Just as Calvino included in his book cities that are desperately uninspiring, like Raissa, a place unaware even of its own existence, I try to show how imaginations are stirred by everything mundane and unpleasant as well as the spectacular. In line with my intent to unfold a paralogy, the work should be viewed as nothing more or less than a commentary on the imperfections, complexities and paradoxes of a counter-world you can easily lose yourself in.

Treating my memories as rhizomatic means the contents of the book should read as an amalgamised entity without too much orderliness: a constant middle without a definitive beginning or end. The only attention given to structure is in the organisation and arrangement of the book's introduction (Chapter 1), its conceptual framework (Chapter 2) and the final remarks (Chapter 10). Otherwise, to fit with the overarching library motif, I arranged the book in a way that unpacks *dangerous* walking without straying too far from 'D' as an alphabetical group. Each chapter (Chapters 3–9) can be read starting anywhere and in any order. Just as they are in my mind, my memories should be examined as if they are in a constant state of becoming and as if they possess no sense of definitive purpose or fixed direction. The book, therefore, is not a tracing but an open map with features that regularly change according to mood, emotion and desire.

References

Bailly, J.-C. (1992) La ville à l'oeuvre, cited in Solnit, R. In: *Wanderlust: A History of Walking*. Granta Publications, London.

Bauman, Z. (1992) *Intimations of Postmodernity*. Routledge, London.

Bech, H. (1997) *When Men Meet: Homosexuality and Modernity*. Routledge, London.

Benjamin, W. (1968) *Illuminations: Essays and Reflections*. Trans. H. Zohn. Edited by H. Arendt. New York: Schocken Books.

Berger, J. (2008) *Ways of Seeing*. Penguin, London.

Blackshaw, T. (2003) *Leisure Life: Myth Modernity and Masculinity*. Routledge, Oxon.

Borges, J.L. (1940/1998) *Tlön, Uqbar, Orbis Tertius*. Viking, New York.

Calvino, I. (1997) *Invisible Cities*. Trans. W. Weaver. Vintage Books, London.

Chatwin, B. (1988) *In Patagonia*. Penguin Books, New York.

Coverley, M. (2006) *Psychogeography*. Pocket Essentials, Harpenden.

Debord, G. (1955) *Psychogeographic Guide of Paris*. Permild & Rosengreen, Denmark.

Deleuze, G. and Guattari, F. (1987) *A Thousand Plateaus: Capitalism and Schizophrenia*. University of Minnesota Press, Minneapolis.

Fermor, P.L. (1977/2005) *A Time of Gifts: One Foot to Constantinople from the Hook of Holland to the Middle Danube*. John Murray, London.

Forsdick, C., Kinsley, Z. and Walchester, K. (2024) *Microtravel: Confinement, Declaration and Microspection*. Anthem Press, London.

Humphreys, A. (2014) *Microadventures: Local Discoveries for Great Escapes*. William Collins.

Kelso, C. (2016) Iain Sinclair – Hard to beat – in conversation with Chris Kelso. *Sensitive Skin Magazine*. [Online]. Available at: https://sensitiveskinmagazine.com/iain-sinclair-hard-to-beat-chris-kelso/

Lee, L. (1969/2014) *As I Walked Out One Midsummer Morning*. Penguin, London.

Lyotard, J.-F. (1984) *The Postmodern Condition: A Report on Knowledge*. University of Minnesota Press, Minnesota.

Miles, B. (2021) *The Backyard Adventurer*. Brio Books, Lidcombe.

Nietzsche, F. (1882/2001) *The Gay Science: With a Prelude in German Rhymes and an Appendix of Songs*. Cambridge University Press, Cambridge.

O'Neill, M. and Roberts, B. (2020) *Walking Methods: Research on the Move*. Routledge, Oxon.

Orwell, G. (1933/2013) *Down and Out in Paris and London*. Penguin, London.

Plate, L. and Smelik, A. (2013) *Performing Memory in Art and Popular Culture*. Routledge, Oxon.

Samuel, R. (1994) *Theatres of Memory: Volume 1, Past, Present in Contemporary Culture*. Verso, London.

Wainwright, A. (1955/2009) *A Pictorial Guide to the Lakeland Fells*. Henry Marshall, Kentmere.

Wittgenstein, L. (1921/1998) *Tractatus Logico-Philosophicus*. Dover Publications, New York.

Dislocation

2

Of Thresholds and Passage. Photo © K.P. Bingham

From the beginning I knew a space of otherness was central to this piece, but it took time to make sense of it, to unpack what it comprises and decide how I might best articulate it. This chapter illustrates my thinking and allows me to expound on why I chose to bind together the notes from my theatre of memory so they sit within a cognitive framework.

With Michel Foucault's (1984) warning about civilizations not possessing boats in my mind after completing a draft of Chapter 7 of the present book, I remembered that *Of Other Spaces* is not the only place the ship metaphor is used. In *Madness and Civilization* which investigates the links between ideas about the great confinement of madness and the Enlightenment project of reason, Foucault (1967/2001) refers to the mythical 'Ship of Fools' as a site that retains its difference and otherness. The madman's voyage is one of ambivalence and uncertainty, and to be associated with it is to become a boundary figure – a transgressor of social order and a form of moral pollution. The Ship of Fools is in no uncertain terms a heterotopic space at the threshold of the everyday world, a site constantly on the move that embodies different attitudes to madness. The idea seemed perfect, and at first it made me think I was dealing with some sort of idiosyncratic heterotopia, a space of personal emancipation that allowed me to explore different alternative ontological understandings of walking dangerously.

It soon transpired that there were problems, however. Foremost among them the idea that heterotopias are collective spaces. As I have explained in greater detail elsewhere (Bingham, 2020), they represent a type of imagined 'community' found within all cultures where likeminded individuals come together in a state of crisis or deviation. While I am naturally influenced by cultures and 'communities', emphasis in this book is on myself and a series of unique circumstances, and of course the thoughts, feelings, perceptions and behaviours that made up my own subjective realities. Another problem, one highlighted by Tony Blackshaw (2017), is that people must have the right 'credentials' to legitimately join the shared space of a heterotopia. It is not enough to possess the necessary skills and knowledge; to genuinely be a part of it people must gain approval from others and then believe in the heterotopia sincerely and authentically. The space I entered in this book was certainly out of bounds to other people, but this is because I chose to be alone. Other people were not prevented from being there, they were simply not around or, when they were, had little relevance to the story other than their absence (Ouvrage Latiremont, for example).

To better encapsulate the idea I was crossing between thresholds, or experiencing a kind of suspension between one world and others, I turned to the concept of liminality. The concept which has its origins in the Latin word *limen* (a 'threshold' between two separate places) connotes a midway state or position in and out of time. Shaped to a great extent by the extensive work of Victor Turner (1969/2017), liminality has come to pervade a wide range of fields and disciplines from religious studies to performance theory, cultural anthropology, travel and tourism and leisure studies. However, as much as the idea of passing through a threshold appealed, the concept posed some problems initially that limited its potential utility. To ensure the concept was suitable as an analytical tool for understanding aspects of the world that are agonisingly confusing, contradictory and incoherent, it was essential I first grappled with it critically.

2.1 Voices of Liminality

To start the critique, it is important to note that liminality is most usually linked with shared experiences of rituals such as those found at music concerts, festivals and sporting events. These rituals not only represent separation from the familiar and habitual, they create cultural domains and social spaces that transcend problems linked with religion, politics, class, race and gender. To entertain the idea that liminality is a dynamic process of constructing shared meanings, beliefs and values, Turner (1969/2017) views joint experiences of liminality through the concept of *communitas*. According to Turner, communitas is found within situations of liminal margin and arises spontaneously within groups sharing a similar position or commitment. It helps people find expression and ways of subverting the rationalistic and utilitarian structures of society. Unlike *civitas* which is described by James Carse (2008) as an inflexible and defensive kind of community, communitas strains towards open-mindedness and therefore entertains cultural and social differences. In the end, what Turner is concerned with is a more powerful sense of belonging than anything implied by the idea of community which, with its promises of comfort, homeliness and close-knit sociability, more often than not disappoints or even disenchants.

Notwithstanding the body of scholarly work that views liminal experience as a collective affair, Zachery Beckstead (2021) reveals that anthropologists have found communitas absent in the rituals they have observed. Revealed instead is the idea that liminality might sometimes involve expressions of individual effort, experimentation and creativity. Indeed, Robert Fulghum (1995) reinforces this idea with his claim that liminality emphasises an individual's existential separateness from others more compellingly than it does instil a sense of togetherness. It is not deliberate, but Timothy Carson (2019) evidences Beckstead and Fulgham's point in his reflective account of a scuba diving incident where he succumbed to nitrogen narcosis and was separated from his diving group. What Carson illustrates is that it is in fact solitariness rather than communitas that is a powerful dimension of liminality.

Another criticism of liminality is that it is most commonly viewed as involving religious pilgrimage. Many scholars have reasoned that the function of a pilgrimage is to facilitate detachment from everyday concerns and reunification between the pilgrim and God. Central to early pilgrimages, René Gothóni (1993) explains, is the figure of the 'foreigner' of Late Latin origin who lived in an alien world outside the safety and protection of Roman territories. Such a journey involved passing from a heavenly homeland, as if they were exiled, to seek out higher goals and truths. Later, the pilgrimage came to mean a journey to a shrine or holy place and the meaning of the term was extended to include the journeys of those travelling to Rome or the Holy Land. The problem with this view in the present day is that liminality is no longer what it once was. As Chris Rojek (1995) has observed, there has been a gradual shift in the meaning of liminality and today it is more commonly understood in relation to spaces and practices of modern leisure. As Rojek argues, liminal zones appeal because they carry the promise of freedom beyond the control of civilised order and leisure situations draw particular interest because they offer innumerable betwixt and between spaces where normal day-to-day life can be temporarily subverted.

A third criticism of liminality is that it can be perceived as an empty concept because it is generally more theoretical than it is ethnographical. The main problem is that when it comes to explaining what is realised during a liminal experience the concept of liminality ultimately remains untheorized since most explanations hinge on its religious, spiritual and mystical antecedents. In other words, one dominant ontological position makes people blind to anything beyond the imprint of a religious paradigm. Although she views Turner's work on liminality as a step in the right direction, in an obituary to Turner following his death in 1984 Mary Douglas (1984) acknowledges that a new discipline (she proposes ethnophilosophy or ethnotheology) is needed to say something valid about mystical experience.

Furthering critique around the empirical depthlessness of the concept of liminality, Tony Blackshaw (2010) turns his attention specifically to Turner. His argument is that in Turner's interpretation, his anthropological roots notwithstanding, liminality evinces little more than the commonsensical argument that human collectives create a shared sense of community spirit, especially when they are relieved from the constraints of day-to-day living. Those who have conducted their own field research, such as Harald Skar (1985) who spent time with pilgrims on his journey to a non-Christian shrine, have also noted that the three-phase sequence in the Turnerian model is consequently not flexible or variable enough to be applied to all liminal experiences. What is missing from the pilgrimage ritual for Skar is an element of tension, hostility and competition that can lead to violent conflict between pilgrims.

Finally, it has been persuasively argued that the concept of liminality has become something of a blanket expression in academic parlance, an umbrella term for an ambiguous or transitional spatio-temporal dimension. Consequently, sophisticated definitions explaining precisely what liminality is are often limited in academic writing or, worse still, they are ignored. Liminality as an analytical tool might therefore be viewed as a brushstroke of an idea that is appropriated merely because it is so broadly applicable. To avoid this kind of criticism, and of course those outlined in the discussion above, I have taken care in the next section of the chapter to outline my definition of liminality. I want to be clear, however, that I am of the view creating a cohesive definition of liminality is a paradoxical idea since the concept depicts a state or condition that is imprecise and lacks cohesion. This is not what I have attempted to do because I acknowledge that the very indefinability of liminality is an essential feature of the concept. My claim, therefore, is that this book is nothing more or less than a medium for understanding liminal experiences that occur as a result of walking dangerously. If this is a study of liminality, which I am convinced it is, it is one that grapples with the idea in a hands-on way, intimately, intuitively and empirically.

2.2   The Liminal Ritual

As it is understood in this book, liminality is a solitary passage but the liminal person does not necessarily know they have entered the state until the true depth of the experience is realised. It is not voluntary, as it would be for somebody challenging the prevailing structure of the world who wishes to express their non-attachment to established cultures and traditions. What I am dealing with in this book is the involuntary kind. These are moments where life thrusts a person into a liminal domain not through willingness or direct choice but by force. Within the territory of this space, the person concerned experiences a form of suspended animation where time and stable and familiar landmarks appear to be lost. With everything in a state of flux, angst becomes the dominant mood and displeasure the critical emotion. Action seems futile as well because immediate peril looks as if it is inevitable and unavoidable.

Clearly the notion of a *boundary* or *border* is central to my understanding of liminality, but I want to be clear from the beginning that the liminal person in this book is figured in the form of the Deleuzian nomad (Deleuze and Guattari, 2010). As vectors of deterritorialization, the temporary life of a nomad is the intermezzo (a performance inserted between the acts of a play) which can take a direction of its own. Nomads of the desert can inhabit places and make them grow as they move between oases which are like fixed points. Yet, their direction and orientation may also be endlessly varied as they often follow rhizomatic vegetation that is temporary and shifts location according to local rains. My understanding of liminality in other words is that it does not represent a fixed outer boundary or a mark of enclosure. I view it instead as a site of transgressivity, a point of entry into another zone that opens, unfolds and allows a person to grow.

My definition of liminality also follows Arnold van Gennep's (1960/2004) tripartite form to some extent, although the emphasis he lays on religion, community and social status has been intentionally disregarded. Additionally, I focus less on the patterned relationship between the three stages and more on the lack of order that is lived through during the liminal period. Like van Gennep, I view liminality as an irreversible one-way passage because a person cannot help but reemerge with an imprint of the encounter left on them (physically, emotionally and intellectually). In other words, I view liminality as a transformational journey. In my mind, though, walking dangerously involves a temporary journey of faith rather than one of certainty since a person may re-emerge with all their parts intact, or they may not. The liminal individual may emerge with rich new knowledge, or with a painful lifelong limp. They could even return with both.

As Chapters 3–9 show, walking dangerously is the quintessential liminal experience. Each journey involved something analogous to van Gennep's notion of the *sacred*, which is a moment of danger and chaos that presents a tear in a person's life or the fabric of modernity. The sacred, for van Gennerp, is essentially a periodic experience of dislocation, disruption and dangerous ambivalence in an individual life, a social context or even in the natural world. Framed around this idea, the notes from my theatre of memory indicate that the classic elements of liminal passage were present on each walk as I found myself moving between the phases of *separation, liminality* and *incorporation*.

Key to feeling separated when walking dangerously is the feeling of displeasure. First, there comes a point on any walk involving possible danger that everyday life comes to a screeching halt. When this happens, a day previously filled with sunshine, fresh air and leisure is suddenly filled with disagreeable things such as risk, uncertainty and confusion. Where a person may have been enjoying themselves, moving with absolute confidence, they find themselves inhibited by an onslaught of information that reads as an unfamiliar language. I might compare the phase of separation to the period of the day known as twilight. More noticeable while camping outside, journeying underground, or driving a car between day and night, this is the moment natural light meets natural darkness. It takes longer than we might first imagine for light to become dark, and to fathom whether it is indeed dark or not. Yet, this is the instant we know the world has transformed. At twilight we lose touch with our normal selves, gaining an acute awareness not only of infinity, mortality, deity but also our very own size.

After experiencing separation, the journey through liminality continues and it is disturbing, depressing and uncomfortable. I would go so far as to say it is a disorienting, paradoxical and ambiguous phase that causes a person to question their deepest beliefs. Social status and identity suddenly mean very little as you begin to feel childlike and vulnerable. There is a sense of surrender as a new way of thinking takes form. For perhaps the first time in our lives we think more seriously about things such as death (specifically our own), isolation and severe dissatisfaction. No longer abstract or suppressed ideas, their inevitability is in the here and now. They are suddenly so real they can be paralyzing.

Unfamiliar emotions spring to life in the liminal zone, especially the painful ones. Anger and fear were the two I usually felt most powerfully. I would find myself feeling furious at my ineptitude, and shocked every time things did not pan out the way expected them to. What I was most angry about was that disaster or misfortune was interrupting my life. Over and above the anger was the feeling of fear rich with the possibilities of displeasure. Since displeasure is a hard sell in day-to-day culture and society, I found I was unaccustomed to allowing myself to feel it. Often, as the liminal experience ran its course, it was painful and exhausting contemplating my deepest held fears but when I did there was opportunity to question everything I had ever believed about life, death and myself. On many occasions I found myself able to replace my fear with curiosity and this was usually when the experience became noteworthy as opposed to frightening. In these moments, walking dangerously was no longer a potential death sentence but a disagreeable existential journey.

In hindsight, if I thought of a liminal experience as unbearably horrible, painful and valueless this is precisely what I would experience. I imagine this is why liminal spaces are too easily described as intolerable places of darkness, personal trauma and suffering. Indeed, Turner (1969/2017) addresses this point with his suggestion that liminality is frequently linked to things such as invisibility, demise and wildernesses. In such places there is danger in that the deeper we go the more terrifying it gets. Those dark experiences, however, would be completely different whenever I accepted that going in deeper was the only way to go. With enough contemplation I found I could become perceptive in the dark. My senses adjusted to the disagreeable and I was better able to contemplate my surroundings.

Once the liminal experience has run its course, a sort of re-entry into the everyday world occurs. By this I mean life goes on. Later, the reader might pause and mull this point over, and rightly so given none of the chapters touch upon this phase in any serious depth. In fact, most of the chapters close at the crux of the event as opposed to a stage of reassimilation. To end in this way was deliberate for I am of the belief that liminality, by its very nature, explains nothing. This is not to suggest liminality is useless, it is to signal that liminal experiences are there to be observed and contemplated. As Bjørn Thomassen (2014) explains, as we probe, reflect and challenge a liminal experience it unlocks the door to a world of contingency where reality itself can be sculpted and carried in different directions. What this book carries therefore is an invitation. It is an invitation extended to the reader for incorporation into indeterminacy, the openness of displeasure, and discomfort and strangeness that drives us forcibly out of our places of contentment and reassurance. With that, it is time to grab our walking boots and get started.

References

Beckstead, Z. (2021) On the way: Pilgrimage and liminal experiences. In: Wagoner, B. and Zittoun, T. (eds) *Experience on the Edge: Theorizing Liminality*. Springer, pp. 85–105. DOI: 10.1007/978-3-030-83171-4_5.

Bingham, K. (2020) *An Ethnography of Urban Exploration: Unpacking Heterotopic Social Space*. Palgrave, Cham.

Blackshaw, T. (2010) *Key Concepts in Community Studies*. Sage, London.

Blackshaw, T. (2017) *Re-Imagining Leisure Studies*. Routledge, Oxon.

Carse, J. (2008) *The Religious Case Against Belief*. Penguin, London.

Carson, T. (2019) *Neither Here Nor There: The Many Voices of Liminality*. Lutterworth Press, Cambridge.

Deleuze, G. and Guattari, F. (2010) *Nomadology: The War Machine*. Trans. B. Massumi. Wormwood Distribution, Seatle, WA.

Douglas, M. (1984) Obituary. *RAIN* 61, 11. Available at: https://www.therai.org.uk/archives-and-manuscripts/obituaries/victor-turner

Foucault, M. (1967/2001) *Madness and Civilization: A History of Insanity in the Age of Reason*. Routledge, London.

Foucault, M. (1984) Of other spaces. Trans. J. Miskowiec. *Diacritics* 16(1), 22–27. DOI: 10.2307/464648.

Fulghum, R. (1995) *From Beginning to End: The Rituals of Our Lives*. Ballantine Books, New York.

Gennep, A. (1960/2004) *The Rites of Passage*. Routledge, London.

Gothóni, R. (1993) Pilgrimage = transformation journey. *Scripta Instituti Donneriani Aboensis* 15, 101–116. DOI: 10.30674/scripta.67208.

Rojek, C. (1995) *Decentring Leisure: Rethinking Leisure Theory*. Sage, London.

Skar, H. (1985) Communitas and schismogenesis: The Andean pilgrimage reconsidered. *Ethnos* 50(1–2), 88–102. DOI: 10.1080/00141844.1985.9981294.

Thomassen, B. (2014) *Liminality and the Modern: Living Through the In-Between*. Ashgate, Farnham.

Turner, V. (1969/2017) *The Ritual Process: Structure and Anti-Structure*. Routledge, Oxon.

Desolation

3

Blackamore. Photo © K.P. Bingham

There is apparently more to the moor than its bleakness. It is said there are compensations and that they can be pleasant, so much so they blind with their charm. Beneath great cloudscapes that are never the same two moments together, they are alive in an endless tapestry of subtle texture and colour. As John Boynton Priestley (1934) said about the people of Bradford in his time-less classic *English Journey*, this is why folk have always streamed out to the moors. No matter how unwelcoming they might appear, something about them continues to glow and attract.

My opinion, however, was starkly different to Priestley's while attempt-
ing the Lyke Wake Walk. Inspired in part by stories of burial mounds and old
coffin routes from centuries ago, the walk was created by Bill Cowley in 1955.
The challenge – a forty-mile crossing of the North Yorkshire Moors from
Osmotherley to Ravenscar featuring 5000ft of ascent and numerous boggy
sections – must be completed within twenty-four hours. Every person who
completes the walk, according to the Lyke Wake Walk Guide (Smailes, 2013),
is eligible for membership as a Dirger or a Witch in the New Lyke Wake Club.
Normally, walkers put together a support team to aid them as there are few
amenities along the way, but I was unaccompanied in my attempt. Having
completed the walk a few years earlier, I convinced myself I was prepared for a
companionless ordeal.

To become as imaginatively uninhibited as possible and make the challenge
seem more authentic, I opted to try it without the aid of digital technology
of any kind. I wanted to experience the violet dusk of the moor, and beneath
wide skies be able to look out across vast plateaus of space and nothingness.
I wanted to notice the little details in my surroundings and experience those
moments so much more vividly than I might in my everyday life. I wanted to
feel exactly like Robert Macfarlane (2007) as he emerges, peat-splattered and
tired, as a bog-person from Rannoch Moor. If I was to follow a marker on a
screen, I would not pause regularly to notice or experience the landscape. I
would not be able to escape the straight lines and garish colours of the everyday world. I would miss intimate things and, consequently, the lure of the
place would likely be diminished. With my mind made up, I left everything
behind except for my map and compass, the clothes I was wearing and a supply
of food and water.

Many people know of the North Yorkshire Moors for its awe-inspiring
expanses of heather, punctuated occasionally by ancient woodland. From the
peaks of its hilltops, as they gaze across the region of undulating and exposed
wildness, people can marvel at a mesmerising tapestry of colour and texture.
Believed to be less dangerous than Rannoch Moor and Dartmoor as the area is
milder in winter and cooler in summer due to its latitude and natural protection offered by the Pennine Chain, it is frequently underestimated for hostility
and danger. In a storm, at night, or alone, though, the North Yorkshire Moors
can be terrifyingly nondescript.

I was walking across Glaisdale Moor as I advanced towards Checkpoint
Four. Slowing me down was a band of wet land. Other than the previous and
present day, it had been raining continuously for almost a week or more,
therefore the notorious 'Boggy Section' of the walk, a section of unstable
peat and myriad natural springs, was waterlogged. At first, I thought of
myself as nimble as I leapt between hags (firmer ground in boggy land)
and thicker clumps of grass, but my feet were eventually taken by surprise.
A concealed void reeking of decomposition managed to draw me into the
earth. It was filled with black water and oily peat and together they battled
to hold my boots in place. It was a struggle, but I was able to pull myself free

and continue in the direction of a nameless road separating Glaisdale Moor from Wheeldale Moor.

As I began my crossing of the Wheeldale section from Hamer at Checkpoint Four, the path was well defined. White painted marker stones guided the way. As I headed further in a generally easterly direction, however, I began to learn the habits and obligations of the landscape. Most of all, I began to understand moor's defiance against straight lines of progress. Going was slow and confusing as I battled my way through springy heather and thick peat bog. My aim initially had been to follow the marker stones together with a compass bearing, but this proved difficult as I was forced to pick my way through a maze of peatland and illusory trail. On several occasions I was certain the moor was patterned with tracks, but it turned out each led nowhere. Having lost the markers, I was following depleted veins that simply stopped dead. Any attempt to pursue them further would have involved negotiating yet another threshold separating one reality from another.

It bothered me knowing I had lost the exact trail, but it was the sheer scale and homogeneity of the moor that seemed to affect me the most, especially my perception of distance. No matter which direction I looked, its sparseness and depth felt incomprehensible. Moments after leaving the safety of the roadside, I happened to glance back only to discover the road was no longer visible. Thinking about it rationally, I must have gone downhill slightly, but I still had the senseless impression that the tarmac had been little more than a figment of wild imagination. So vast and barren was the space within which I was moving that when I finally caught a glimpse of Blue Man-i'-th'-Moss (a medieval boundary stone), it seemed as though I was barely advancing at all. Like an explorer approaching high mountains that loom across the skyline and never appear to get any nearer, my feet seemed to be falling exactly where I lifted them.

Out on the Moor, nothing had moved for a long time. For a few hours or more I had walked and discovered no one. Other than my own footsteps, there was no living sound. Humankind might have been a thousand miles away; such was the profound separation from the everyday world. Such openness and the complete absence of connection with other human beings can be nearly impossible to find in the everyday world, but in the empty seas of moorland it endures. I have experienced openness like this before but every time it still fills me with astonishment. For a while I gazed longingly into the vast expanse in the hope I might spot someone, yet between myself and the slight bow of the horizon stretching as far as the eye could see there was little to be seen or heard.

Several miles back, there had been numerous signs of humanness. I was touched at many points by its presence. The cairn at the summit of Botton Head, the highest point in the Cleveland region, marked a clear point of orientation; a landmark to aid navigation and route finding. The nameless road, too, was a direct link back to civilization. Even the paths themselves, marking the persistent passage of human beings, cut everywhere across the landscape like rough scars. Flecked all over with exposed stones worn smooth from centuries of traffic and rain, they serve as a reminder of the mastery of the patient walker. My Ordnance Survey map and compass were also clues the land crossed had been carefully measured, named and recorded. Not an inch remained unchecked by faint blue lines, or contours and eastings.

Now, as I looked around, rolling moorland extended as far as the eye could see. There were no paths. As I surveyed the landscape, I began to slip into the trap of exercising an imaginative bias against the moor. Just as Daniel Defoe (1724/1778) viewed the moors above Chatsworth House as an extended landscape of waste and howling wilderness, a pang of fear swallowed any ability I might have had to interpret the terrain as anything but dismal, empty and limitless. Like Defoe, I began to contemplate just how easy it would be to lose my way. My enemy, it seemed, was the immensity of the moor with its concealed hazards and unpredictable behaviour. In that moment, I understood why the imprint of religion on the moor, with its abbeys, barrows and boundary crosses, is together ruined and weathered. There is no place for God on the moor, nor language that excels in penetrating such an abominable world.

Covered in dense woodland once, in the sense that it was a mosaic of woodlands shaped by wild animals rather than a closed-canopy forest, the moors as they appear today are featureless. Marked only by ancient mounds and grassed-over stones, seemingly historic as though they were once Roman or Celtic forts, there are innumerable remains of farm buildings and sheep folds that have sunk into the ground. There is dereliction all through this land, rot that is centuries old and set in well. Laboriously built fences and walls, now windswept and broken down by rain and ice, were erected at some point to carefully divide the land into smaller, manageable plots but many of them have become indistinguishable as one space of heather or bog is usually unrecognisable from another. The moorland then, with its threatening, amorphous forms is more a symbol of destruction than it is of inspiration or beauty.

No doubt, it was the same landscape I was seeing that inspired Emily Brontë (1847/1987) gothic novel *Wuthering Heights*. Drawing on the otherness of the moors of Yorkshire, Brontë uses the desolate landscape as a mirror for the characters' strangeness, immorality and their unrecognisable human actions. Ultimately, it is the sheer bleakness of the landscape that draws the key characters (Heathcliff and Catherine) into their own chaotic version of culture and society. Full of passion and conflict, the pair are synonymous with the wildness of the rugged moorland as they strive for disconnection.

As it turns out, I was less about finding disconnection than I first envisaged. Visiting the North Yorkshire Moors alone had seemed like a good idea when I was making plans in my centrally heated house. Yet, once I had achieved the task of finding myself alone I began to wonder whether I had been entirely sensible embarking on the walk in this way. Projections of Victorian fears and phantasmagoria were troubling me as I paused to consult my map. Where I was stood, I thought, I was probably one of the remotest people in entire country. Miles away from the nearest house, my decision to travel alone served only to heighten my imagination and bring the experience of desolation into sharp focus. In company with others, I might have debated how far we had left to go, or which route we thought was the most direct. I would have focused, that is, more on the conversation than my surroundings. Alone, however, I had no one to disengage my attention from the landscape. Nor did I have anyone to rely on. If the motionless trauma and turmoil of the empty moorland decided to unleash its terrors, there was nobody to listen out for my cries for help.

Notwithstanding the voluminous nature of the open moor, the environment as I noted earlier could not have been anymore noiseless. For a while there was neither wind nor traffic. Even the birds were silent. The serenity of such a silent world could have filled me with pleasure, and indeed it has on many occasions, but I was unable to admire it in any enjoyable way this time because of the calamitous nature of the silence. In the calm there was a deadly stillness, a silence so profound I could have heard a pin drop against the ground. In *The Shadow Line*, Joseph Conrad (1917) describes such a feeling as the captain envisages the end of his ship in the absolute calm of the tropical sea. I could feel it too, the anticipation that something with the power to end all things could happen. I could feel something calamitous lurking in the background, waiting to silently overwhelm, and I knew it would ambush without a stir.

It was only later that the silence of the moor transformed. With the same emptiness of a desert, the landscape gradually revealed itself as an inexhaustible reservoir of subtle noise and sensation. In the company of others sounds of this kind would normally have been undetectable, but being unaccompanied gave me access to noise that is infinitely smaller and born of emptiness. To my left, the rasp of heather moving stiffly. To my right, the subtle murmur of waterlogged earth. And much later, when I finally came across a tree, a survivor of the ancient world rather than an escapee of a conifer plantation, I found myself able to listen to its melancholy song. Its leafless limbs deeply furred with moss flowed up into the air and it was just there, at their tips, they whispered with dying breath. The sounds lasted no more than an instant, before being dispersed into the air to be degraded by the gentlest of breezes.

Also revealed in the emptiness of the desert was a reawakening of my eye's capacity to offer a superior vision of the totality of being. As Jean Baudrillard (1986/2010) explains, a desert's emptiness can be a visual thing as well because it shows how human or natural constructions that intercept the gaze often corrupt the perfect reach of a person's vision. Once this is realised, Baudrillard explains, the desert can emerge as more than a space from which all substance has been removed. Hence, just as silence is not what remained when all sound had seemingly disappeared, the horizon of endless desert that at first seemed as static as a photograph turned out to be a motion picture of infinitely high definition. In fact, almost every bit of the undergrowth across the motionless moor, from its vast swathes of heather to its moor and cotton grasses, could be seen responding to an eerie wind that was imperceptible against my own skin.

The longer I allowed my eyes and ears to animate the emptiness and silence all around me, the more a desert of loathly nakedness arose. And with it the hushed work of erosion steadily revealed itself. Removed centuries ago to make way for grazing and pasture land, there were few trees or flowers to fill the air with brightness. More successfully accomplished in silence was the deep melancholy of stone, partially decayed vegetation and twisted heather stem. With such sombre emotion, the silent work of the moor gave rise only to the gloom of devastation and desolation.

With the landscape suddenly alive with imperceptible sound and movement, I began to appreciate why moorland is often associated with dark myth and legend. From Crazywell Pool on Dartmoor (see: Salmon, 2023) – a bottomless pond that calls out the next parishioner to die at dusk – to the Black Dog of the North Yorkshire Moors (see: Walker, 1988) that serves as a warning of impending doom, myths abound. I knew it was my imagination speaking, but I was almost convinced I was not alone. Skulking on the horizon, there was something or someone out there. As a boy, I used to experience the same feeling when I was sent to fetch a newspaper or milk from my Nanna's village shop. To get there I had to walk down a narrow-gravelled cut lined with high walls and tall conifers that seemed dark and foreboding. I felt a presence on my shoulder every time I walked the route and now that same presence had rejoined me. Perhaps it was the *Barghest* Nicholas Rhea (1985) mentions in *Portrait of the North Yorkshire Moors* that foretells death to the people of North Yorkshire. Perhaps it was a sign of impending disaster. Whatever it was the presence did not remain long, and having only glimpsed the beast for a fleeting moment I could live with the knowledge I had been granted life rather than death.

I rejoined the trail as I neared the end of Wheeldale Moor. With the remains of Wheeldale Plantation in the distance to my left, I proceeded for a while along a narrow stony path. By now the sun had disappeared and the day was becoming grey with great sagging spans of newly forming cloud. Rain was imminent, I was certain of it. All that was needed to shatter the heavy clouds and realise the full force of their fury in a deluge was a gust of wind. As before, not a soul was about. Other than a solitary buzzard crying desolately, its song a plaintive high-pitched mew as it beat up against the wind, no other life stirred. There is only one other time I recall feeling such isolation and this was in New Zealand's so-called Death Valley. I did not have far to go now until I reached Eller Beck Bridge on the A169, the main road over the moors from Pickering to Whitby, but it was impossible to believe the path would ever end.

A few hundred metres from the Grade II listed bridge, a little-altered structure built before 1840, the landscape changed. The rough stone path I had been following widened as it gave way to compressed gravel. Still technically on the moor, I had re-entered its civilised space carved out for crowds of families wanting to picnic and walk on Sundays or Bank Holiday weekends.

Now the North Yorkshire Moors has been passed to an authority tasked with conserving and enhancing the natural beauty, wildlife and heritage of the area, a second kind of desolation can be witnessed. To borrow Glyn

Hughes' (1975) description, as the moors have been given National Park status a Boy-Scoutish amateurism upsets the landscape. Gone are notions of wilderness or wildness; preserved as a place for relaxation, tranquillity and escape, there are welcome signs now, together with tarmacked toy-like bridges, bus stops and notices outlining rules and codes of conduct. The moors have been given charm that attracts people, but it is cultivated charm that is (once it is noticed) hard to get away from. As Hughes put it in his account of the woods at Hardcastle Crags in West Yorkshire, such charm is a bit repulsive. I might go so far as to say it is a thorn in the side of the North Yorkshire Moors. It causes or disguises, depending on the way you look at it, greater bleakness and emptiness than the moors ever had to begin with.

References

Baudrillard, J. (1986/2010) *America*. Verso, London.

Brontë, E. (1847/1987) *Wuthering Heights*. The Great Writers Library, London.

Conrad, J. (1917) *The Shadow Line*. Doubleday, Page & Company, New York.

Defoe, D. (1724/1778) *A Tour through the Whole Island of Great Britain*. Dent & Sons, London.

Hughes, G. (1975) *Millstone Grit*. Victor Gollancz, London.

Macfarlane, R. (2007) *The Wild Places*. Granta Books, London.

Priestley, J.B. (1934) *English Journey*. William Heinemann, London.

Rhea, N. (1985) *Portrait of the North Yorkshire Moors*. Robert Hale, London.

Salmon, A. (2023) *Dartmoor*. Culturea, Hérault.

Smailes, B. (2013) *The Lyke Wake Walk Guide: The Official Book of the New Lyke Wake Walk Club*. Challenge Publications, Barnsley.

Walker, P. (1988) *Murders and Mysteries from the North Yorkshire Moors*. Robert Hale, London.

Discontent

4

The Wainwright Summit. Photo © K.P. Bingham

The night before setting off from St. Bees, the official starting point of Alfred Wainwright's (1987/2017) 182-mile hike from the Irish to the North Sea, I was camped on the seafront with some whisky and a copy of *Civilization and its Discontents* (Freud, 1930/2002) in hand. First published in 1930 as *Das Unbehagen in der Kultur*, Sigmund Freud's book provides an in-depth examination of conflict that occurs between societies and their individuals. What I was beginning to realise as I neared the end of Chapter 3 is that Freud is exploring the problem of hostility towards civilization. His central argument rests with the paradox that the civilizations people create to protect themselves and ensure survival and happiness are in fact the cause of extensive discontent. The conflict arises, Freud suggests, because cultures demand conformity and constructive ends while individuals struggle to repress their own urges and yearnings.

While societies and cultures persist in heightening feelings of discontent, wild places generally seem uninterrupted in the way they attract people's attention because they are perceived as the antithesis of modernity and urbanisation. In the pantheon of literary icons, Henry David Thoreau (1854/2023) is famous for praising wild mountains and winter forests as some of the last sources of freedom. For Thoreau, direct contact with wilder places simplifies life as the pressures of conformity can be escaped. This is why he went to the woods in *Walden*; he wanted to confront the essential facts of life and live so sturdily as to rout all that is not life. In many ways, I wanted the same. When I initially set off from St. Bees, vivid mountains and valleys sprang to mind. In the freedom of them, I imagined wide skies and fiery sunsets over glistening tarns.

What I neglected to consider, however, is discontents, and Thoreau's warning that too much distance from society can be lonesome, oppressive and unpleasant. To feel such things, he suggests, is to doubt whether the nearness of others and civilization is not essential to a happy life. The source my discontent on the walk discussed in this chapter was the weather. Cut off from civilization by rolling fog, I was reminded as I made my way from High Stile to Haystacks of the rawness of wildness and ancient fears of the unknown. I was reminded as well of things I sometimes take for granted, such as the familiarity of everydayness and the nearness of safety.

I had never really given much thought to it before, but after reading Kate Rew's (2022) book *The Outdoor Swimmers' Handbook* shortly after returning from the Lake District it occurred to me that cold can manifest in myriad forms. For most, cold as the presence of low temperature is a hostile condition. It conflicts with inclinations to feel comfortable in ways that are both physical and emotional. Until a relationship or close connection is established, the most common experience of cold is an unpleasant sensation of chilliness, sometimes accompanied by shivering and a desire for insulation and warmth. When a relationship (good or bad) with the cold is formed and it is understood more intimately, it taps us back into the wild and wordless logic of the feeling self.

Occasionally, we might say it is tepid. When I am tepid, I would suggest I am neither warm nor cold. At the height of summer this might be pleasant, enjoyable even, but at any other time there is a peculiar sensation something is missing. When I am chilly, I feel mild sensitivity to the cold. I might say a moderately uncomfortable freedom from heat is experienced. Feeling brisk is different altogether. Cold when it is brisk is not unlike wine with a sharp and pleasant taste. There is a sense of energy and liveliness to it and for this reason it is deeply invigorating. A distinctly unpleasant type of cold, however, is the bitter cold. To experience bitterness is to feel a violent assault on the inner body. The outside body barely has time to register the bone chill since it easily bypasses all flesh and clothing. With each breath it is unscrupulous in the way it leeches warmth from the soul. Numbing cold can seem less severe, but it is equally as unpleasant in its own way. This kind of cold has a bite, so fierce it can seem hot and fiery as bare skin smarts and burns.

As I began my descent of Haystacks, a cold trickle of water managed to find its way down the back of my neck. I shivered involuntarily and pulled up my hood. I was feeling damp cold. Damp cold is unpleasant in its own special way because it is before anything else miserable. What it lacks in severity, it makes up for in discomfort. The slightest movement is a reminder that water has soaked through everything to the skin. Damp clothes are heavier when wet, so they cling and inhibit movement. Worse still, as wet clothing is less effective at trapping warm air it steadily cools the body, sometimes to the point of causing hypothermia.

My experience of Haystacks was shaping up to be very different from what I had expected. When I first decided to include the fell in my walk, I had begun with Wainwright's (1955/2009) description of it being the best fell top of all for '[its] beauty, variety, and interesting detail, for sheer fascination and unique individuality', and for '[its] great charm and fairyland attractiveness'. Not quite a mountain as it is just shy of the requisite two-thousand feet, the summit of Haystacks sits on a short rocky spine overlooking several tarns with rocky shores and miniature islets. The rocky spine is itself a mass of flow banded andesite lava rock thrust up by ancient eruptions that has slowly been cracked and splintered by frost, ice and the power of flowing water. My crossing of it was part of a 50-mile walk from St. Bees to Penrith. My aim was to complete the walk within twenty-four hours, but the way things were looking I was not sure I would make it any further than Honister Pass. Wainwright, it seemed, had deceived me with his romantic portrayal of the fells.

The rain was silent against the surface of a nearby tarn. I thought I was adjacent to Innominate Tarn, the spot where Wainwright's ashes were scattered by his wife, but I couldn't be certain. Enveloped in thick, wetting cloud with the veiled sun sinking low in the sky, visibility was poor. Like Nan Shepherd (1977/2014) as she ascended the second highest mountain in Scotland, Ben MacDhui, there were moments the cloud was so thick I could do little else but stare into a pot of whiteness. I was disheartened to be denied a view, but very quickly the feeling was replaced by disconcertment when I noticed there was a ghastlier white materialising on my lefthand side. As Shepherd describes, this was the white of non-life spreading and swallowing from an invisible abyss. Being careful not to lose my footing on loose rock, I ushered in the power of ignorance and turned my attention to the clamminess of the air.

After a day of continuous light rain, my beard had become wild and unruly. It felt wet and coarse as I tried in vain to stop the tangled hairs creeping into my peripheral vision. My shoulders felt damp and uncomfortable as well. I was wearing an expensive waterproof jacket, hundreds of pounds worth of Gore-Tex actually, but it was starting to hold onto water rather than repel it. What many people do not realise is that Gore-Tex requires regular maintenance to reap the benefits of its waterproof properties and that it will over time degrade, especially when substances such as sweat, dirt, suncream and insect repellent build up within the microporous membrane. My jacket, it seemed, had reached such a point of degradation sooner than I would have liked.

In the Lake District, prevailing westerly winds come from the Atlantic Ocean. With them they bring moisture on their breath. At sea, the winds accumulate vapour until they reach the maximum amount the volume of air can hold and when the air reaches the Lakes its rugged fell mountains force a rapid cooling effect as it travels upwards. This causes moisture to condense into rain. According to Julian Mayes and Karel Hughes (2014), the technical term for this process is orographic precipitation and it is the reason why the Cumbrian region is so mercilessly wet. Today's clouds had reached me and as they moved further inland, they were shedding droplets and an autumn chill.

As I worked my way towards Dubs Bottom, the site of an old slate quarry wedged between the peaks of Fleetwith Pike and Great Round How, the sky began to darken. Up on Haystacks, where visibility had been non-existent among the cloud, the rain had been fine and misty. Now, with the cloud more dispersed, a restless wind was building. Every now and then a phantom lash of cold, dense air would nearly rush me off my feet. The weather was changing; brushing against the rugged valley sides, the wind was generating friction. As I understood it, it was friction causing the wind to slow and then speed up again. Notwithstanding the science, the gusts made me feel uneasy. The ferocity of each burst was extraordinary and alarmingly unpredictable. No sooner was there commotion lashing out in great whips of wind, an instant later it might disappear and give no clue as to when it might reoccur.

As the first fat drops of rain began to hit the already sodden earth, I decided to make for Warnscale Bothy. Nestled on the edge of a cliff, the small building is perfectly camouflaged at the bottom of a pile of discarded slate. As I hastily slipped my map and phone back into a waterproof case, the rain grew heavier. Within minutes a downpour had started. The rain that followed seemed to defy gravity and fall with more force than I thought possible. I had known ahead of time that heavy rain was imminent, and I had prepared accordingly, but was still taken aback by its intensity. A blanket of water was thrown over previously visible things so that the world was suddenly intermittent and fragmented. Only the violence of the occasional gust would part the deluge enough that some of my surroundings might reappear for a moment or two.

I stuck with a boggy trail, hoping it really was a trail and not an animal track, and took care to keep the river on my righthand side. I continued for a troublingly long time. Long enough that I started to worry I had walked past the bothy. Desperate to gain some sense of direction, I paused to scour my surroundings. Visually, I was staring into nothingness. Just ahead, however, I could hear rain drumming with a deeper, steadier sound than it would make against the ground. With water dripping from my hood, I paused a moment longer and strained my ears. There was something to my left. Promising sounds were spreading through the nothingness, enough to give me a sense of perspective. That was when I saw it, a small mountain hut carefully nestled in the slate pile.

As I stepped inside the bothy I was met with relief. The air was cold and dank, but it was respite from the conditions outside. Trailing water on the flagstone floor, I moved to the middle of the room to look around. There were two benches for sleeping and a good-sized fireplace fitted with an old cast-iron stove. A blackened frying pan lay on the stone hearth, along with a metal shovel and a brush. The mantel bore an empty matchstick box and what appeared to be an old candlestick holder. There was also a window. Normally it might have framed Haystacks, Crummock Water and Buttermere perfectly, but presently it framed only vertical sheets of water. Under the pressure of the gale outside, I could hear the window frames flexing. The wind was pushing hopefully against the panes, and every now and then it would throw a heavy splatter of rainwater as a reminder it wanted to join me inside.

Hoping to get a fire going so that I might dry off a little, I searched the bothy for wood, kindling and a lighter. My search for supplies proved fruitless, however. Disappointed, I sat down on one of the benches to determine my next move. As I sat to eat some food, I slowly peeled off my waterproof jacket to inspect it for dry patches. Examining the saturated lining with my torchlight, I caught out of the corner of my eye water vapour rising steadily from my damp body. Although I discovered there were fewer dry patches than there were wet ones and was conscious my damp clothes were growing colder and more uncomfortable, I settled against changing into my spare set of clothes. I was due to complete the walk within twenty-four hours so there seemed little point in changing while I was keeping the pace up. The rain, I decided, was not going to ease anytime soon so before I grew any chillier or could think about changing my mind, I pulled up my hood and set out once again for Honister Pass.

Outside, the wind was noticeably colder and the rain still falling in a continuous stream. However, even though night was fast approach and I only had around twenty-minutes of daylight left, visibility seemed to have improved and I could better comprehend my surroundings. Starting in the direction of Dubs Quarry, one of the many slate mines in the area, I followed what I presumed were the bumpy remnants of an old haul road. Damp cold was pressing fiercely now and before long I was shivering. These were not surface level trembles, they were deep convulsive shakes. The damp cold, I realise, was quickly becoming bitter cold. Nothing human seemed to belong or work out here. I was, to borrow a fantastic quote by Robert Macfarlane (2007), in a land 'thrown up by fire and survived by ice', far away from safety, familiarity and predictability. Just as Macfarlane experienced on the summit of Ben Hope, I felt no epiphany of companionship or relation with the land. I had entered a place of broken slate that seemed hostile to my presence. Wildness that deprives a person of the means to provide for themselves was bearing down on me. There was nothing to suggest I was welcome here.

For the next hour or so I got lost and made painfully slow progress. The rain had picked up shortly after leaving the hut, so much so it had become a living fabric. If I had wanted to, I am certain I could have reached through and used my fingers to part the cascade. I needed to find somewhere to take shelter and see out the remainder of the storm. I cast about for sheltered ground, somewhere to set up my bivouac bag, but could find none. Darkness had swiftly descended upon me and transformed a previously known landscape into the wild unknown. Disassociations swarmed out of the darkness, new shapes and forms I was certain had not been present earlier, and I seemed to enter a new topography. The path was not where I had left it moments earlier, and as for Honister Pass, it could have lay in any direction. With her suggestion that imaginations come to be increased when the setting of the sun occurs, Elisabeth Bronfen (2008) talks about the disorientation I felt. As sense of distance and measure changes, she explains, and contours become blurred, new orders of connection establish themselves. It is possible, therefore, to become disorientated but equally more aware of a landscape's threatening and fascinating effects.

In the midst of my disorientation, I came across a rough pile of slate with a narrow length of flat ground at its base. It was hardly the best place to wait out the weather, but my options were limited as long as the dreamlike world I had entered remained paralyzingly eye-fooling. Depleted of motivation and energy, I unfolded my bivouac bag as quickly as possible and did my best to stuff my sleeping bag inside without it getting too wet. Keeping my boots on, which made wriggling difficult, I pushed myself inside as deeply as I could manage. Using my rucksack for insulation against the cold ground, I lay awkwardly for a while in a reasonable state of warmth. The ground was more uneven that I had supposed, but for a while I sunk into a restless sleep.

It could have been minutes or hours, I cannot say for certain, but I eventually jerked awake. As my eyes adjusted to inexplicable shapes skulking in the darkness, I noticed I was trembling. The earth, having caught me off guard, was drawing me inside. As it leeched warmth from my body, I curled up tightly like an animal. I felt cold down to my bones. Exposure is a sinister thing, especially when dampness is added to the mix. It can quickly bring on uncontrollable shivers as the body tightens and relaxes in rapid succession to combat hypothermia. I grew concerned as I lay in the darkness and wondered whether it was time to accept defeat. I was cold beyond belief, yet the thought of leaving my sleeping bag did not appeal to me in the slightest. Knowing the trembling would intensify if I abandoned the shelter, I stalled for a while longer. I knew, of course, I was merely delaying the inevitable. With the weather worsening and hail starting to gather as ice around the bivouac, reality set in. I knew it was time to bail.

Now, my only concern was reaching the safety of Honister Pass where I would be able to make my way into the much calmer – or so I hoped – Borrowdale valley. And so, suddenly I found myself behaving as Samuel Taylor Coleridge (1800-35/1954) did on his descent of Broad Stand; I engaged in a form of gambling he claimed had become an addiction as I set off to find the first possible point of descent. My unlaminated map, now a pile of mush, was unreadable so finding a track or other symptom of safety was impossible. Relying, therefore, on little more than good fortune, I followed a vague trail to what I believed was Striddle Crag. Unable to find a route that seemed possible with tolerable ease, I straddled the top of the precipice as my search continued. I must have missed the small beehive cairn on the summit of Fleetwith Pike, and the public footpath leading across Fleetwith Edge, because my route in the end was far wilder and more scrambly. Like Coleridge, I suspected that I ought not to go on since I knew one wrong step would probably kill me, but I continued anyway. The thought of turning back into the raging hail seemed more unbearable, as was any notion of reascending the rock face. I could feel the closeness of civilization in the direction I was heading, so I kept going.

References

Bronfen, E. (2008) Night and the Uncanny. In: Collins, J. and Jervis, J. (eds) *Uncanny Modernity*. Palgrave, London, pp. 51–67. DOI: 10.1057/9780230582828_3.

Coleridge, W.T. (1800-35/1954) In: Coburn, K. (ed.) *The Letters of Sara Hutchinson*. University of Toronto Press, Toronto.

Freud, S. (1930/2002) *Civilization and Its Discontents*. Trans. D. McLintock. Penguin, London.

Macfarlane, R. (2007) *The Wild Places*. Granta Books, London.

Mayes, J. and Hughes, K. (2014) *Understanding Weather: A Visual Approach*. Routledge, Oxon.

Rew, K. (2022) *The Outdoor Swimmers' Handbook*. Rider, London.

Shepherd, N. (1977/2014) *The Living Mountain*. Canongate Books, Edinburgh.

Thoreau, H. (1854/2023) *Walden*. Walter Scott, London.

Wainwright, A. (1955/2009) *A Pictorial Guide to the Lakeland Fells, Book Seven, the Western Fells*. Frances Lincoln, London.

Wainwright, A. (1987/2017) *Wainwright's Coast to Coast Walk: From St. Bees Head to Robin Hood's Bay*. Frances Lincoln, London.

Delinquency

5

A Ship of Fools? Photo © K.P. Bingham

It was 2015 and I found myself walking the outskirts of one of New Zealand's largest cities. I was by the entrance of a disused boat yard, a site I had been told was formerly owned by the brother of a Russian billionaire. Some research I conducted few months later revealed this was not completely true, but while I believed it, it made for a good story. On the property were several one-hundred tonne yacht hulls, abandoned because the company had gone into liquidation years ago, and I was eager to photograph them. The largest of the superyachts, despite it being only half-finished, was alone estimated to be worth $18 million. All that lay between the boat graveyard and I was a single obstacle, one that has been used since the tenth millennium BC. Between us there was a gigantic wall.

© CAB International 2026. *The Book of Walking Dangerously: Notes from a Theatre of Memory* (K.P. Bingham)

As a phenomenon that has played a major role throughout human history, from the Walls of Jericho to the Great Wall of China, to Hadrian's Wall, the medieval walled cities of Europe, the French Maginot Line and Donald Trump's Mexican border, wall building might support impressions of order in an otherwise insecure world. Viewed in this way, walls bear resemblance to mechanisms of safety and security as they are used to resist imbalances in societies between communities and transgressors. In reality, though, walls only appear orderly. While they may have been built primarily for defensive purposes in the ancient world, the roles they play today have become multifaceted. In the twenty-first century they are used more commonly as overt tools of oppression, a means of controlling commerce and impeding freedom of movement.

Understood today primarily as a means of defending the resources and objects of those who have them from those that do not, the word 'wall' carries a strong sense of restriction, discrimination and general hostility. It is, as Nick Hayes (2020) eloquently puts it, a technology of division that imposes a simplistic binary logic. Walls not only separate one from the other by preventing free movement, but they also inflame antagonisms, evoke violence and legitimise difference. As a universally understood symbol of authority, everybody is aware, consciously or not, of the power they both protect and project. As well as serving to protect resources and objects, walls segregate lower-level humans from members of the higher orders. They reinforce the orthodoxy of social hierarchy as doxa.

As far as their physical properties go, however, walls are almost always ineffective and impractical. As fortifications, they can be breached or easily broken, and the longer they are, the harder they are to defend. In the end, most crumble to dust or survive only as tourist attractions. The Berlin Wall is a prime example. Designed to keep Westerners from entering and undermining the socialist state of East Germany, the wall made it impossible to cross freely between East and West Berlin. Yet, despite featuring myriad watchtowers, barbed wire, mines and gun emplacements, some 5000 East Germans are still believed to have crossed between the two territories. What is more, the fragments that remain in existence today, following fall of the wall in 1989 which led soon afterwards to the collapse of the Soviet Union, have become touristic objects for viewing and photographing. Quite simply then, physical aspect of a wall does not work.

What walls really represents is an idea. Residents of Berlin called it *mauer im kopf* (the wall in the mind). According to Peter Schneider (1982), this is an invisible barrier constructed in a person's psyche that takes longer to tear down since it exists long after the removal of the physical wall. For many people this is a moral conundrum centuries in the making and it encourages them to avoid stepping out of line. The wall between the abandoned boatyard and I had a similar effect. Vandalism and graffiti showed me the wall was all but useless. But, because the idea of a barrier remained I was reminded that land beyond was charged with exclusion.

The part of the city I was in was an industrial zone, a grey part of the world consisting of factories, warehouses and dusty tarmac. Doing my best not to look too conspicuous as I loitered near the entrance of the old yacht maker's yard, I gazed for a while at the obstructing wall. I was unsure what to do next. Featureless and the same dull grey as the rest of the area, it was roughly the height of two human beings. It did not look too difficult to climb, but with taught lengths of barbed wire lining the top there was a clear message on display.

After waiting patiently for a break in the traffic on the main road, which was busier than I would have liked, I began my climb into the murky ground of trespass law. With no real strategy in place for negotiating the barbed wire, I scrabbled with it as I tried to stop my trousers from snagging. My movements were deliberate but frustratingly slow as I lifted my first boot on top of the wire and paused momentarily to regain my balance. I was on the wall long enough to feel self-conscious about being spotted, especially by pedestrians, before I could swing my other leg up and jump down onto the ground below.

After landing with a thud, I immediately set off in the direction of a set of steel warehouses. As I crossed the wide-open yard, I passed one of the half-built superyachts but did not dare pause to photograph it for fear of being stopped. Had I not been so anxious, I might have marvelled as I do now at the power of the barrier I had crossed, and how its presence had the authority to cast a spell of submission. I was, I remember, flushed with discomfort and uneasiness and felt a deep-rooted sense of being morally wrong for crossing a distinct line into the abstract realm of private land. What I also recall, however, is the feeling I was being wronged since I seemed to accept without question that I was engaged in deviant behaviour even though the land on which I was stood had, only one-hundred and seventy years earlier, been publicly accessible and without imaginary lines conjured by colonialism and privatisation. The previous inhabitants of the land had viewed ownership very differently. As Pippa Salonius (2024) explains, born of the earth's womb Māori considered their association with land more as 'belonging to' rather than having 'rights to own'.

In a word, I found myself forced against my will into the role of the '*Other*'. Inside the physical and metaphysical boundaries of the yacht makers, I carried the threat of the wrong classification and so I was something to be fought against and expelled. This is not to suggest my 'Otherness' has ever forced me beyond the physical boundaries of a town or city, or that it prevents me from pausing for a while in one place. In this sense, I am not an 'Other' in everyday social space perhaps as a refugee might be because I am very much part of the everyday. What I am though, in my ordinariness, is a stranger to other city dwellers and together we are all suspected of carrying danger. As Bauman (2003) explains, capitalism is responsible for the mass production of Zygmunt strangers and 'Otherness' as it fought against guardians of ethical duties and put cost-and-gain calculations above obligations and commitments for other human beings. Freedom from strangehood, as Bauman argues, can be found only among those occupying the highest positions in the social hierarchy, or those who are driven by entrepreneurial needs and ambitions. Consequently, in the twenty-first century freedom means little more than freedom for private investment, accumulation and profit.

I entered the warehouse by slipping beneath a broken roller shutter door. And there, towering above me, was a white multi-million-dollar superyacht almost entirely sheathed by scaffolding encapsulation. Together with feelings of disquiet as I feared being caught, I was swept away with a sense of pleasing, almost euphoric, overwhelm. I could not stand and gawp for too long though as my fear of encountering security was bordering on paranoia. As I set to move again, I instinctively stooped low to avoid being seen and set my sights on climbing aboard the yacht. Urged on by untested hope rather than clear destination, I began my journey through an unstructured place of tangled poles and uneven boards. Whether it was like this because it was unfinished, partially demolished or because it had been impacted by an earthquake, I did not know; the fact remained, nonetheless, that the makeshift walls, ceilings and floors throughout the warehouse were plentiful but paradoxically abstruse. Like a wanderer in a desert, who knows only of the trails marked by their own footsteps which can be blown away any moment, I walked not knowing when to stop or for how long.

When I eventually reached the upper deck and could step completely off the scaffold, it occurred to me that two opposing façades of life, as they do in Italo Calvino's (1997) city of Moriana, had suddenly come into view. What I had uncovered is the ontological violence of the aesthetics of revulsion set against the pure passage of the beautiful. In the region of the beautiful, Dylan Trigg (2006) explains, a person's gaze may be serene but too often it is also deeply melancholic. Melancholy is felt because perfection can be faceless, banal and powerless. Certainly, the yacht was a magnificent reflection of wealth and elegance, especially below decks, but it became increasingly monotonous the longer I remained on board. Intriguingly, what I found richer and more exquisite was the deterioration of the place. Revealed and weaving in complexity were the possibilities of the revulsive and unaesthetic.

What Johann Wolfgang von Goethe (cited in Freud, 1930) said of life in general, that nothing is more difficult to bear than a succession of good days, is also true of the aesthetic of beauty it seems. Compared with the dreariness of uniformity and changelessness, the chaos of movement, particularly of decay and dilapidation, can ring out as beautiful. Unpacking a similar idea in his meticulously detailed discussion of ugliness, Karl Rosenkranz, (1853/2015) encourages his readers to think about how *any* movement in fact, whether it be a crashing wave that sprays whirlwinds of foam into the air with raging cheer or a mountain range whose misshapen trees dance dreamily above those that have fallen long into the perfumed distance, can be alive in epic and dramatic poetry.

Belonging to land now rather than the sea, the superyacht was a place where shapelessness, incongruity and ugliness took precedence over the pleasures of splendour. Lacking definition where definition ought to have been as it was layered throughout with grime and dust, the yacht had become both nebulistic and undulistic. The wavering and uncertainty of the vessel's boundaries contradicted the very concept of its design and shape, yet this contradiction was satisfyingly ugly. If Rosenkranz, (1853/2015) was to explain it, he would no doubt point out that there is nothing natural whatsoever about the unnatural. A predator or poisonous plant, he argues, might commonly be known for, even characterised by, their beauty but in their natural form they are really self-dirtying, incestuous and wily. To be appalled by such words, or to view them as misdeeds, he suggests, is iniquitous since they belong to the world of thought and intellect. The unnatural, by contrast, which cannot intentionally break laws, lacks the same power of consciousness and freedom of will.

Just as the super yacht had both a beautiful and ugly face, I too was experiencing two sides of myself, or two different lives. On a day-to-day basis, I do my best to conceal the 'ugly' portion of myself. As best as possible I cover up the 'Otherness' and temporarily remove my lust for it from thought and memory as I try to live with composure and civility. But occasionally my opposite side is rediscovered, a part of myself that embraces, perhaps even comprises, rusted metal, dust covered surfaces and rotten paintwork. I may long to fix such 'ugliness' in my everyday life, but really it represents a version of myself I wish I could be more often, a self I should set out to further understand and appreciate that dwells in imagination, wildness and present and future possibilities. This side is almost always abandoned in favour of aesthetics, the home of the preferred tourist where order, stability and some degree of grandeur come to be expected. It leaves the defenders of 'normality' confused about what might amount to a fuller existence and what exquisiteness can hide among the seemingly rotten foundations of life.

My 'Otherness' and people's unacceptance of it became all the more apparent twenty-minutes later when the police arrived. Before I knew for certain they were there, I had sensed something was wrong. An eerie silence had descended upon the warehouse, the same silence that occurs in the ocean before a ferocious storm or after a loud sound has shattered a period of stillness. It was a car door closing that prompted me to peer through one of the gaps in the side of the warehouse. It turned out the door belonged to a police car. Right away I panicked, but before I could react the lights in an overhead office were turned on and a figure appeared at a windowed door overlooking the warehouse floor.

The moment I heard keys being fumbled into a lock was when I dived for cover inside the superyacht. Realising I was trapped between two groups of police, upstairs and outside, I lay flat against the deck and crawled madly until I reached a ladder. I descended as quickly as possible and then bolted towards a loose flap of metal that was partially covering a fire exit. Being careful not to snag my camera bag on the sharp metal, I squeezed through and without looking back proceeded to walk across the yard towards the exit and main road. My plan, hitched together only moments earlier, could not have been simpler. I would try to exit through the main gate which was now conveniently wide open as calmly as possible to avoid attracting attention. I almost made it, but as I approached the road two armed police officers stepped out from behind a stationary digger. They were just as surprised to see me as I was them.

What is interesting is that on every occasion I have ever been caught trespassing it has never been the owner of a property I have encountered. Rather, it has always been a police officer, private security guard or a warden. These are the people it falls on to protect private land from invasion by the delinquent and so they are eternally cast against the 'Other'. Sarcastic, sardonic and often point-blank rude, to borrow Hayes's (2020) apposite description of gamekeepers, the approach of police and security typically hinges on an exaggerated hyper-masculine type of aggression fuelled with indignation. They like to give the impression they are justly retaliating to an act of wrongdoing because in the eyes of law enforcement officials trespassing inside private property, whether it happens to be abandoned and dilapidated or not, is an act of deliberate aggression against landowners who are automatically cast as the victim.

With their gazes firmly locked onto mine, the two dutiful police officers began their cross-examination. As they started with their questions, they were joined by three other official-looking figures who proceeded to form a tight circle around me. They demanded to know what I was doing, and when they did not believe I was an amateur photographer I was asked to show proof of identification so they could check my credentials. The images on my camera, too, were subject to close scrutinization and they pressed me to show exactly what I had taken photographs of. With batons, tasers and pepper spray conspicuously displayed on equipment belts and enthusiasm to use them manifest, I suddenly felt disorientated and fearful. Faced with an inadequately paid security guard, my instinct might normally have been to run. Now, I barely dared to move. My pulse raced, thumping hard in my ears as I watched the police closely. My breathing was shallow as the air was being forced through barely parted lips and an extremely dry mouth. Many questions circulated in my mind as the intense scrutiny endured. Whenever I spoke the words caught clumsily in my throat.

In his work on manipulable delinquency, it was Michel Foucault (1961/2009) who explored the idea that police and felons occupy the same world. This was precisely my thinking as I speculated about what would happen to me next. Although some of Foucault's analyses read as a sympathetic endorsement of neoliberalism, in some of his major works such as *History of Madness* and *Discipline and Punish* his ideas are guided by a critique of capitalism and it was these ideas that came to mind while I was at the mercy of the police. In *History of Madness* for instance, he suggests that the exclusion of the insane was the pretext for the surreptitious enclosing of other unproductive parts of the population. A key feature of his argument is that the modern state tolerates and ignores the misdemeanours and criminal transgressions of the rich and powerful because they contribute to economic expansion. By contrast, the state over-polices and over-imprisons the less-productive portions of the population because their contribution is deemed inadequate. The police-prison system therefore normalises what should be considered abnormal and by acting as a moralising power it helps people distinguish between who is and who is not a delinquent. Without doubt, I was cast in the role of the unproductive delinquent.

In the eyes of the police, I had broken the treaty of the 'tourist'. Having fallen foul of the law, I had wilfully chosen the plight of the 'vagabond'. Tourists, as Bauman (1993) reminds us in *Postmodern Ethics*, pay for their freedom. To gain the right to spin their own webs of meaning and experience the pliability of space, they engage in a contractual deal and this involves compliance and willingness to make commercial transactions. For a tourist, there is a world to be lived pleasurably but decorously. This is the world of aromatic restaurants, exotic thrills and hotels with subservient staff, all of it waiting docilely for the tourist to derive aesthetic meaning and pleasure from it.

As I waited in the shadow of a superyacht for the police to decide what to do with me, I remained motionless and reflected. Two features that unite tourists and vagabonds, I thought, are that they both move through the spaces other people own and that they have become the dominant moulds that shape the patterns and practices of quotidianity. Together, the two metaphors set the standards of happiness and success in the everyday world. The danger of course, as Michel Foucault (1984) concludes in his paper on utopias and heterotopias, is that 'in civilizations without boats, dreams dry up, espionage takes the place of adventure, and the police take the place of pirates'. In this warning about mobility, we are reminded that imaginations disappear when dreams dry up; that ideas of adventure are too easily scrutinised; and that the story of pirates as one of freedom and liberty can, without great difficulty, be superseded by the tales of policy makers and law enforcers who have the power to decide how probity and delinquency should be defined.

References

Bauman, Z. (1993) *Postmodern Ethics*. Blackwell, London.

Bauman, Z. (2003) *City of Fears, City of Hopes*. Goldsmith College, London.

Calvino, I. (1997) *Invisible Cities*. Trans. W. Weaver. Vintage Books, London.

Foucault, M. (1961/2009) *History of Madness*. Trans. J. Murphy and J. Khalfa. Routledge, Oxon.

Foucault, M. (1984) Of other spaces. Trans. J. Miskowiec. *Diacritics* 16(1), 22–27. DOI: 10.2307/464648.

Freud, S. (1930) *Civilization and its Discontents: Volume XXI*. Hogarth Press, London.

Hayes, N. (2020) *The Book of Trespass: Crossing the Lines that Divide Us*. Bloomsbury, London.

Rosenkranz, K. (1853/2015) *Aesthetics of Ugliness: A Critical Edition*. Trans. A. Pop and M. Widrich. Bloomsbury, London.

Salonius, P. (2024) Mother, earth, sister moon and the great forest of tane. In: Bintley, M. and Salonius, P. (eds) *Trees as Symbol and Metaphor in the Middle Ages*. Boydell Press, Cambridge, pp. 12–65.

Schneider, P. (1982) *The Wall Jumper*. Penguin, London.

Trigg, D. (2006) *The Aesthetics of Decay: Nothingness, Nostalgia and the Absence of Reason*. Peter Lang Publishing, New York.

Disconcertment

6

Christchurch Basilica. Photo © K.P. Bingham

On 22nd February 2011, an earthquake measuring 6.3 on the Richter scale caused substantial and widespread damage across New Zealand's second largest city, Christchurch. With countless buildings estimated to have been affected and large areas of the city without power, water and sewerage, a state of civil emergency was declared. Within days support teams from all around the world arrived, but it was only when recovery work began that the true extent of the surface cracking and soil liquefaction was revealed. As the removal of wreckage commenced, official damage assessments revealed that hundreds of buildings, many of them important heritage sites, were unsalvageable. The earthquake had made the land so unstable it was predicted many would be destined for demolition.

Included in the long list of historic sites impacted by the disaster was the Cathedral of the Blessed Sacrament, a renaissance-style basilica often compared to Saint Paul's Cathedral in London. Regarded as one of the finest examples of church architecture in Australasia, the site served as the mother church of the Roman Catholic Diocese of Christchurch. As well as weakening the structure throughout and ruining most of the stained glass, the earthquake completely obliterated the building's two front bell towers and destabilised the green copper-roofed dome above the sanctuary. Of the front façade, the only key features to survive were the fine Corinthian and Ionic columns and a large cross with two angels abreast keeping vigil.

It was 2014 when I first walked into Christchurch. I was lured into the city by destruction. At the time I was a student researcher investigating the relatively new phenomenon of urban exploration, and it was early in my trip I found myself adjacent to the same fallen basilica I had set eyes on in the news. For a while I loitered on a public footpath across the road from the cathedral, partly to avoid looking suspicious whenever police and security vehicles passed by, but also to pluck up enough courage to engage in some trespass in broad daylight. After deliberating what might happen if somebody caught me, eventually I goaded myself to cross the road. Feeling more willing to enter the building once I was nearer, as casually as possible I slipped beneath a flimsy wire fence intended to deter would-be trespassers and walked briskly in the direction of the building. My heart was racing and my hands and legs shaking as I made a beeline for cover.

Tucked behind a large plinth after gliding up the front steps, I paused for several seconds to gather my thoughts and regain some control of my trembling limbs. I wondered whether anybody had seen me, and if they had how likely they would be to call the police. As I deliberately stalled and procrastinated, my eyes performed a sweep of my immediate surroundings. To my left, thin shards of metal protruded from heavily damaged chunks of stone. Overhead, just above a double set of doors, thick cracks could be traced. Not unlike contour lines drawn on a topographic map, they ran all across the cathedral's façade indicating where changes in the structure were developing. To my right, a tall section of wall in the corner was stained with obvious signs of decay. It could have been moss, algae or mould, I could not tell which. All I knew for certain was that something green was oozing from some quite significant gaps in the stonework and that I was being teased by an all-too-familiar aroma of dampness.

When I felt the coast was clear, I entered through one of the large wooden doors nearest to me. It was unlocked and slightly ajar. From outside I had been awestruck by the basilica's crumbling towers, cupolas and domes, but once inside the feeling was magnified two-fold. It was not like any cathedral I had ever seen before. In fact, it was not like any cathedral on earth. I felt the bite of cooler air as I took my first few steps past an empty reception booth. Not stopping, I headed towards a trolley that contained a collection of dusty hymn books. Although their covers were still deep maroon in colour and they were neatly organised, I could see their pages beginning to wrinkle and crease.

As I stepped into the central nave, I noticed that the smells of wooden furniture and moisture were heavy in the air. The effluvia was the kind that is unmistakable in an abandoned building but also oddly refreshing. Seating to my left and right, most of it arranged in rows, still faced the direction of the Holy Table. Among the many surviving chairs were the marred, those crushed by huge pieces of masonry shaken loose from the walls or ceiling. The chair nearest to me, just on the right, was now occupied by a stone block the size of a television from the early 90s. Although the impact had buckled the backrest, somehow the debris remained suspended in the air.

Ahead, beyond the rows of chairs, I could see a gaping hole in the ceiling. Where there was once a copper dome, gloomy clouds coiling in the daytime sky could now be seen. Directly below the ragged opening lay an altar, but it was like none I had ever seen before. At least two stories high, this holy platform of rubble was towering. It was guarded on each side not by angels or venerations of the Virgin Mother but massive statues of smashed stone. Where candlelight once cast a warm glow against smooth marble and gilded surfaces, streaks of daylight danced against weeds protruding from fragments of hard-coloured masonry.

Without doubt, there was strange beauty to be found in these ruins. This seemed odd to me at the time as I felt a profound surge of sadness should have been more appropriate. What I felt nevertheless was something similar to Edith Wharton (1915/2022) as she watched Rheims Cathedral burn shortly after it was bombed during the Second World War. In her report of the event, Wharton describes herself stood in a dull provincial square before a structure entirely wrapped in flames. It was a scene so strange and beautiful, she suggests, that words to explain it could only be found by searching for them inside the inferno. Although my encounter was after the event, to have walked into a place like the Cathedral of the Blessed Sacrament was to imagine in the very same way as Wharton. Taking the place of her deep tints of umber, burnt sienna and carmine were macabre blacks, earthen browns and heavy olives of Cladosporium decay.

For all the beauty, I was in the knowledge that there was something profoundly disconcerting about everything I was witnessing. To borrow Wharton's way of putting it, I was gazing at the beauty of disease and death and there seemed to me a special kind of corruption and wickedness in it. I knew that each perfectly carved stone was cracked to the core, that the statues would inevitably crumble until they were dust, and that there were signs in all places a cathedral was dying around me. The disconcertment I was feeling seemed to spring from the idea that the unreal was unravelling and revealing itself to be more real than reality itself.

A name has been given to the feeling . The influential thinker Sigmund Freud (1919/2003) referred to it as the *uncanny*. It occurs in moments when something familiar reveals itself to be strange and previously unknown. Without doubt, all around me there were signs of the divine and the diabolic; clear, interweaving contradictions between a space that was simultaneously majestic and commanding but also an alien double. It was inconceivable in such a sacred space that I could see cracks in the columns lining the nave, and that an ornate ceiling of embossed zinc looked ready to be peeled away from the rest of the roof. Yet, the destruction was there and clear as day. Concern over the presence of a higher being or of the spirituality of the place should not have been a concern for a nonbeliever such as myself, but something divine still clung to me. As a result, I was too afraid to stand and gawp for long, afraid of my steps echoing too loudly and of the grandeur of the desecration and destruction. I had entered the carnage of a world that was all wrong, an uncanny world that transforms views on permanence and transience.

Coincidentally, a few weeks before writing this chapter I had been reading about spiritual beings known as Mondongs who are said to sing intimidating songs in the ochre mines of the Australian outback (Hunt, 2019). This story returned to me, almost immediately, when I recalled my experience of the strangeness of the uncanny. When I first read the tale, I was perplexed that rational people – experienced miners and anthropologists – could believe in the existence of small, dark-skinned beings who would suddenly appear like shadows before disappearing again just as quickly. But the stories began to make more sense reflecting upon the crumbling basilica because I realise I shared a similar experience. The miners and anthropologists were entering an impossible place, one carved into the gloom of the underground. Simply being involved in the act was enough to further disturb the natural, contributing to its inevitable transformation into the unnatural. It was perhaps the sacrilege, I think, that was responsible for causing uncanny feelings of presence and the plaintive and haunting wails of song.

I stopped still in the nave, pausing to better take in the chaos. After several seconds, I began to rotate on the spot until I was facing the entrance. I spotted a gallery overhead and it featured a large pipe organ built in 1878 by the famous Birmingham organ builders Halmshaw & Sons. An ordinary sight inside a cathedral, except that the scene was in no way normal. Rather like the melting clocks presented by Salvador Dalí in *The Persistence of Memory* (1999), the twisted pipes of the longstanding instrument were folded over a low gallery wall. In the same way Dalí uses the clocks to convey impossible, dreamlike scenes, and force his viewers to encounter something indescribable, undefinable and unknowable, the pipes made me question once again what was real. In the space I had entered, the concept of the cathedral was not functioning in a familiar or reliable way. It had proven itself unreliable and therefore unknowable.

Interestingly, the same feeling returned to me several years later when I turned on the radio to discover there was a fire in the capital city of Paris. The fire, it was announced, was tearing through the great cathedral of Notre Dame. At the time, reporters suggested that the blaze, after striking quickly and uncontrollably, was able to gather such immense power and ferocity it was likely the building would not survive. As I watched, reporters' comments seemed prophetic as live video footage from the scene showed an inferno so large it engulfed much of the roof and central spire. Lost for words, I could not comprehend how such a monumental building could have survived the Middle Ages, the brutality of the French Revolution in the 1790s and two World Wars yet fall at the hands of a discarded cigarette or an electrical fault. To witness the embodiment of medieval Paris crumble in an instant, everything from its intricate carvings, historic paintings and priceless collections, was to feel as though Dalí had been at work once again. The scene, as it had been in Christchurch, was in every way inconceivable and unknowable.

I snapped out of my trance. There are certain places, I thought, that you leave never expecting to see again. I decided I was in one, an architectural splendour built for the glory of another time, and before the chance was gone I wanted to see what the cathedral looked like from above. The gallery with the organ was my best bet, so I headed for a nearby stairwell. As I walked my footsteps echoed loudly against the hard floor, filling the cool depths of the cavernous building with the song of untidy movement. I passed through a set of gates which creaked faintly as I drew them open. The iron pickets, I noticed, were a peculiar mixture of arrow tips and spear heads. Such objects seemed strange in their pious setting, contradictory even. Also strange, having anticipated it would be stone, was the cast iron staircase I found. I felt the narrow spiral structure belonged elsewhere, not among such an extraordinary phenomenon of masonry.

As I ascended the stairs, I noticed large chunks of metal were missing from several treads. One or two even lay whole at the bottom of the stairwell. They had been sheard off the central column by great hunks of falling stone which had then shattered into dozens of pieces across the floor. It dawned on me, only after seeing the carnage, that I was perhaps inside one of the cathedral's ruined towers. Tentatively, I worked my way upwards. It was impossible to use the staircase in a normal way, so I made my own course. The route should have sent me in a counterclockwise direction, but I was spared the boredom of having to move in circles as I weaved up, over and around absent pieces of metal.

Ducking beneath an intact pane of glass that had been shaken loose from its frame, I stepped into a new corridor. There was more rubble strewn across the floor in this part of the cathedral, and the decay so endemic walls that were once pristine white were now wholly darkened green. Simultaneously the colour of rejuvenation and putrefaction, the green teased me with ambiguity. Fertile with life and death, what I found here was a new tapestry. Both powerful and uncanny, the image worked to re-sculpt my memory of God as luminous revelation to withering loss. The layer of moss had stitched itself firmly against the cathedral like a second skin and I now bore its looming shadow. Everything, from my clothes to my skin, was tinged a sepulchral green as I entered an eerie world that might normally be suppressed by the flame of a fuller divinity.

I was not long in the corridor. Eager to dodge the colour causing more curious upwellings of uncanniness, I moved towards a tall wooden door. A plaque fastened to the lintel above read: CHOIR ROOM. I reached out to grab an aging brass handle. Expecting resistance, perhaps some swelling of the door in its frame, I was surprised to find it opened easily. I stepped inside with fervour, but a gut feeling stopped me dead in my tracks. The choir room was missing, just as it might if the building had been hit by a wandering bomb. Where the room should have been there was open air. It should not have been possible, but I could see and smell Barbadoes Street and all of Christchurch beyond.

I recall feeling like Laurie Lee (1969/2014), the famous English poet and novelist who fought against Franco's Nationalists in the Spanish Civil War, as he stood before the Cliff of Crows in the Roman-Iberian city of Segovia. Set at the foot of the cliff, Lee describes a sedate little church of the local Virgin and a strolling priest who seemed strangely drawn to the place. As he stands with the priest and gazes at the granite rock, he is informed they are looking at a cliff of blood. This is a site, he is told, where accused felons, adulterers and heretics were tossed from the summit into the gorge below. Just like Lee, what I had found was not a sedate place of worship but a bruise in contradiction of it. The same birds from the cliff, those belonging to the world of the damned, were perched on the ragged edges of the destroyed room. This was a sure sign of the uncanny world I had entered, for the dry voices of the birds only ever haunt exhausted crevices or bloodstained faces. Where there are no birds, there are no ghosts with godless souls.

Stepping back into the corridor, I continued walking until I reached the organ sent from England. With pipes resembling Dalí's clocks, it was almost certainly in an unplayable condition. What I had found was a reclusive creature, one left behind and forgotten all-too-quickly by fleeing humans. Somehow it had survived the destruction and, except for the pipes and a few broken keys, remained intact. Just as intricate and complex as a clock, this was more than a box of whistles and dusty notes. It was a misplaced body capable of producing celestial and soothing harmonies and triumphant proclamations. Gently, I slid my fingers over the soiled keys. Fighting back an urge to push them, I headed for the gallery's edge.

From where I was stood, the gallery could be followed in two ways as it extended down either side of the nave. The righthand side seemed to lead to a small wooden pew. It was perfectly positioned, I thought, for viewing destruction. Things were different on the lefthand side. There, the gallery sloped unnaturally. Thick cracks ran through the base of the walkway giving it the integrity of a broken pier. I decided not to think too much about the integrity of the section I was standing on. Instead, I turned my attention to the scene before me.

The carnage and catastrophe sucked me in as I looked out from the balcony. What I was witnessing was a mighty basilica forced to transform. Before me, destruction revealed a new cathedral growing steadily from broken stone, shattered glass and flora. The cathedral was dichotomous, suspended uncannily between the divine and the diabolic. It should have breathed life, after all it still looked like a place of worship. The problem is that it no longer was. Rather like something undead, such as a zombie or a vampire, that functions and looks as though it is still living the cathedral excited a sense of unease. There was a strong inclination to still accord respect. I did not make too much noise or engage in vandalism, nor did I disturb anything. Yet, I could not help but feel a diabolic presence not only capable of abolishing all rules and rituals but also all value. Having seen a palace reduced to its constituent parts, lifeless heaps of stone, marble and glass, the disconcerting mark of destruction was left firmly imprinted on me. This, I reiterate, was a world all wrong.

References

Dalí, S., Zeri, F. and Dolcetta, M. (1999) *Dalí, The Persistence of Memory*. Nde Pub, Ontario.

Freud, S. (1919/2003) *The Uncanny*. Trans. D. Penguin, London.

Hunt, W. (2019) *Underground: A Human History of the Worlds Beneath Our Feet*. Simon & Schuster, London.

Lee, L. (1969/2014) *As I Walked Out One Midsummer Morning*. Penguin, London.

Wharton, E. (1915/2022) *Fighting France*. SAGA Egmont, Copenhagen.

Desperation

7

The Natural Underground. Photo © K.P. Bingham

I was searching for a cave whose entrance is less than obvious. It is found inside Eldon Hill Quarry, a site used extensively for limestone excavation between 1950 and 1999. The quarry itself is set in a limestone hill that was formed by powerful geographical forces capable of forcing a bed pure calcium carbonate into a dome shape. For many years the area was used as pastureland for rough grazing, but a large proportion was lost to excavation work in the twentieth century. Lying just 350-metres to the south of Eldon Hill and part of the same carboniferous limestone is Eldon Hole. Known locally as the abode of the Devil and described by Hobbes (1678) as one of the seven wonders of the Peak, it is said to be the deepest pothole in the area.

My interest on this occasion was not in Eldon Hole. That's a story for another time, perhaps. Instead, my attention was drawn to Sidetrack Cave, a system discovered in 1994 by quarrymen. Although the cave looked promising when it was first unearthed, permission for further exploration could not be granted as the quarry was still a working site. Over the next few years some of the newly discovered cave was lost as the rock face (and subsequently the cave entrance) was gradually worked back, but when quarrying operations ceased cavers were allowed to return. Following a short period of digging on one of the upper terraces in August 2002, gaps in the mud were discovered. The first led into a dry fossil phreatic passage, choked a few metres in, which would later be named Alsop's Cave. Forty metres further along the terrace, a second entrance was discovered. Smaller, but seemingly more promising, this became known as Sidetrack Cave.

It was 2020 when I first attempted Sidetrack. Still relatively inexperienced as a caver, I decided to go alone as I was struggling to convince my usual caving partners to join me. It was late November, furiously cold and close to midnight, so hardly surprising the others were uninterested in going caving. Completely unaware the cave is better accessed by abseiling into the quarry, I entered from the bottom. Knowing I needed to reach the uppermost terrace and that there would be no fixed protection, I combed the lower levels hoping to find easy scrambling routes. It took me longer than expected to gain any height; everything I tried pinching with my fingers crumbled to dust, and everything I stepped on seemed to explode under the pressure of my weight. In between gritting my teeth and holding myself as closely as possible to the rock face, I made painfully slow progress.

As I neared the uppermost terrace, my right hand fumbled in the darkness. I was trying with increasing desperation to search for something to grasp. My left hand was pinning me as closely as possible to the rock, and I was all too aware that my bodyweight was being supported almost entirely by my left leg on a miniscule foothold. To stay balanced, I had to position my right strategically for counter pressure. As a consequence of fear rather than fatigue, my supporting leg began to tremble. I held the position for a while, up until I was certain I was about to fall. Knowing as a matter of urgency I needed to move, I lunged for what looked like a bombproof ledge. It broke immediately, and I watched as a large chunk of rock peeled loose from the wall. A violent stream of rocks and lumps of mud followed. On impulse, I clasped the rock more firmly with my left hand and somehow managed to cling on.

Having grasped too tightly, my fingers convulsed painfully. I was convinced, as I loosened my hold a little and waited for the discomfort to subside, that a rock collapse was imminent. When I finally set out to start climbing again, I discovered I was paralysed by fear. Frozen in place, I willed my eyes to reveal a safe route onto the final terrace, but I found it difficult to distinguish things clearly in the darkness. I had a headtorch strapped to my helmet, but its beam was too bright against the limestone face. This and the fact I had limited range of motion with my head made me feel disorientated. Teetering on the border of the known and unknown and being and not-being, I yearned for escape. I wanted nothing more than to slip into the superficial safety of thoughtlessness and inaction. It must have been the adrenaline pumping hard around my body that saved me but by some miracle, or perhaps sheer panic, I managed to finish the climb.

Once I was safely on the terrace, I paused to look around. A sweep of my headtorch exposed a rock-strewn platform. Large enough, I think, to carry a two-axle truck, it was dotted with boulders and patches of low-lying vegetation. I felt comforted having light again, now I had the freedom to cast it in any direction I pleased without dazzling myself. It gave greater detail and perspective, and it drove away feelings of uncertainty by giving me a tangible sense of place and context. Gaining poise, I turned to begin my search for the cave entrance. Surprisingly, it only took a few minutes to find. This was, or so I felt at the time, my first bit of luck of the night.

I entered the cave slowly, conscious I was passing into a special place where the outer and inner worlds meet. Cavers refer to this as the *twilight zone*, an area of a cave that is mostly grey in the daytime and where the rock is only faintly outlined. As it was after midnight there was no sunlight, so signs I was moving between light and dark dwelled only in the air. In the twilight zone the air is incongruous. Here the muddy aroma of the Kingdom of Darkness (see Bingham, 2023) seeps up from below while the sweeter scents of the surface world linger momentarily. On a warm summer's day, the air is wonderfully air-conditioned. On a cold winter's evening, as it was on this occasion, it feels warm and hospitable.

It was the cultural anthropologist Victor Turner (1973) who developed the phrase *betwixt and between* to capture the essence of his concept of liminality. For Turner, the betwixt and between involves great ambiguity because a person experiences a spatial separation from the usual and habitual. By this he means people can transcend the limitations of class, gender, politics, religion and even geography. In my mind, the twilight zone is precisely this kind of space. As the shadows grow weaker, you can sense everything you are about to lose, and you know that in a few short steps the world will insist on its paradoxes and uncertainties. It is not Cerberus or Hades who are passed, not a guardian of the underworld demanding payment in exchange for keeping the dead from the living, nor Auguste Rodin's *Gates of Hell* where we are told all hope must be abandoned. A threshold is crossed but this is the unadulterated threshold of *darkness*. To enter it is to step into darkness that is darker than anything we might normally encounter. This is a threshold where eyes cannot acclimate regardless of how long a person waits, hence it is conveyed largely through emotions which affirm an alternative (dis)order of things.

I was headed in the direction of a small chamber known as 'Little and Large's Airbells'. This is a section, after 89 metres of flat-out crawling, where it is finally possible to stand up. I was little more than 10 min into the cave, however, when something inside my headtorch popped. The light immediately went out and I was thrown into total darkness. Having foolishly abandoned my tacklesack near the entrance, I was left without a replacement light source. At first, I was outraged at my own ignorance and stupidity. I wondered how this could have happened to me, how the situation could even have been possible, but this feeling was quick to dissipate.

Doing my best to quell abounding panic, I squinted in the vain hope my pupils would dilate and soften the darkness. Nothing happened of course, no pale outlines of rock emerged, nor was there any glimmer of light from behind. My heart rate quickened, and I was struck with the overwhelming sense I could not breathe. Still not quite believing what had happened, I waved my hand frantically in front of my face. I implored my fingers to make ripples in the fabric of darkness, but nothing happened. The black curtain surrounding me was impossible to move. Involuntarily, I had entered a world of absence and it filled me with a sense of unreality. Although my body had not moved an inch since the torch had gone out, being short of light and tangible features meant I started to lose sense of my bearings. With frantic movements I scrabbled to locate a rock, something that could be hurled so that I might rediscover the last wall I had seen. Unable to find anything, the fear of entrapment grew stronger. To avoid losing my bearings any further, I decided in that moment it was safter to remain motionless. As I lay completely still, my ears pricked to the sound of my heart rapidly throbbing against the ground.

For a person used to living in an ocularcentric world that is media obsessed and designed specifically for the eyes, I found my inability to see utterly debilitating. I was defeated, or so it seemed, by an alien world of impenetrable night. This should not have come as a surprise because I am aware that scholars as early as Plato have viewed the human eye as the mind's eye and the gateway to divine inspiration. Ultimately, as John Berger (1972) says in *Ways of Seeing*, it is the privileging of sight that has not only created but sustained cultural infatuation with the idea that seeing establishes our place in the everyday world. As for pervasive darkness, it has long been associated with peril, discomfort and inconvenience. Nighttime in medieval towns, Roger Ekirch (2005) explains, was a dangerous time because murderers and thieves lurked beneath overhanging timbers in excrement laden streets. In times of widespread superstition as well, darkness was conceived as a realm where ungodly forces congregated. From spectral appearances to troglodytes, witches and invisible gases, all kinds of sinister things have persisted in the gloom.

I wish I could suggest the darkness interrupted my own light infatuation and suddenly moved me in some profound and insightful way as it did for the young poets of bardic schools who were sent to compose poetry in completely dark cells (Raymo, 2008), or that it helped me understand something like Śūnyatā which, in Buddhist philosophy, is emptiness that can be used as a means of gaining perception about reality (Sheehy, 2019). All that happened, however, is that I experienced the horror of being made blind.

Blinking seemed to make the darkness worse. Blinking made me feel as though my eyes and body were failing to connect, as they might if my visual cortex had suffered some kind of catastrophic damage. I could sense my eyelids move, but there was no evidence of them ever having blinked. For the first time in my life, my eyes were utterly useless. There is only one other time I recall my eyes failing to work and this was shortly after my father died. I had travelled to the Isle of Man and was camping just outside the small town of Ramsey in the north of the island. On the first night, I woke in the early hours to find I had been buried alive. My eyes opened to darkness and when it failed to dissipate horrifying thoughts wormed down inside my body. As they chewed their way into my inner architecture, my heart thundered against my ribs. Feeling as though the air was thin, I clawed blindly at my tent until I found the zip and was able to burst out onto a silent field.

For a few moments, I stared ahead into obscurity. I was unsure what to do and quite taken aback by my reaction to the darkness. Some cavers suggest that being in a cave without light is like being dead, but this was not the case for me. I was certain my body was still my own. What I felt instead was that I was terrifyingly close to whatever lies beyond the margins of the earthly world. I was at risk of straying into the unearthly and indistinguishable world of the mind. It was Sigmund Freud (1923/1961) who famously argued that the id – the unconscious instinctual component of personality – is a mostly negative and inaccessible part of a person's personality and on reflection this is perhaps what I was risk of discovering. As Freud would have said, at my own core there was a cauldron of chaos boiling with excitation and a dark self. Deep inside me was the energy of desire and a primeval need to survive. In every way it was irrational because I knew escape might be possible if I crawled backwards. Yet, just as I had reacted in the tent, something impelled me to claw at the earth with my fingernails.

It had only been a few minutes but as I lay motionless and uttered obscenities, I felt I had already remained in darkness too long as I was sensing with the sound of my voice the contours of the cave. Just as John Hull (2017) was able to use the acoustic experience of rain to gain a sense of perspective in his garden, each time I spoke or moved cascades of sound seemed to drip from the walls to unveil invisible space. What I found together strange and disconcerting was that I had moved from a world filled with vivacity into a world of nothing but my own activity. I was the sole source of being, bringing it into and out of existence, because when I stopped crushing silence would immediately return. Everything else, I noted, had passed out of existence; the mud as a symphony of rich browns, impressions and moulds of past life in the rock, and even pools of murky water, none of it was really there. I disliked this new and unfamiliar reality. I missed the clarity of the surface world, along with the logic of ordinary consciousness.

Desperate to escape, I started edging my way backwards. My hope was that I might reach the entrance if I was cautious and took my time. As I was unable to turn my head to look over my shoulder, I had no clue what was behind me, so before I could shuffle and gain ground I was careful with every movement to feel for empty space with my feet. I proceeded like this, wriggling my boots exploratorily over the cave floor and gaining distance of only a few inches at a time, for what felt like an eternity. What I found challenging, despite having encountered few obstacles on my way into the cave, was that in reverse there were now countless boulders, obstructions and strange turns to contend with.

Such was my disorientation that on several occasions I managed to convince myself I had backed into an alternative passage and was mistakenly receding further and further into an alternate underground void.

Moving made my helmet and oversuit rasp vociferously as they rubbed against the cave. The noise gave me better perspective in the confined space, but the thick material prevented me from feeling the cave with my body. Twice I stopped dead in my tracks when my face rubbed up against something cold and damp. I knew it was likely to be mud because its petrichor-like aroma lingered in my nostrils, but my imagination was working hard to convince me that whatever I was touching was neither safe nor recognisable.

Another challenge made greater by my helmet and oversuit was my heightened awareness of physical pressure. I might compare it to being woken by a full bladder in the middle of the night and trying to reach the bathroom without switching on a light. There were moments, just as there would be in a pitch-black house, where I would instinctively freeze or raise an arm to protect myself whenever a physical presence was felt. Too often I found myself gritting my teeth, usually when jagged rock probed my ribs or I thought my head was within striking distance of a wall. Although I was restricted in how far I could move, my head would recoil every time from whatever the presence was. Outside the cave, during the day or perhaps on a well-lit street, this would have been an impossible experience since sensation of pressure is unnoticeable in the chaos of the everyday.

The impact of bursting into the outside world was so immediate it took me by surprise. All of a sudden the night air was striking my face. It swamped my lips and my ears before flooding my mouth with its sharp renewal. In an instant I had undergone a transition from dark to light, having moved away from abstraction into the concrete realities of moonlight. In the lustre of the lambent moon, now visible because the cloud from earlier had moved on, bushes and shrubs on the quarry terrace were clearly silhouetted. Behind me, a towering face of pallid rock stretched as far as the eye could see. Stark and unending, the rockface offered only one remarkable feature – a small arched opening at its base. The hole breathed darkness. It also breathed presence, the uncompromised sublime presence Ann Colley (2016) talks about that has not been weakened by the reflective discourse of philosophers, poets and tourists, which is compounded of the power, the oppressiveness and the unknownnesses of nature and the apparent feebleness of being human. What I had found was a portal that leads straight into to horrors of the natural underground, an opening where the ugliness of darkness is sensuously penetrating and desperately profound on all kinds of emotional levels.

References

Berger, J. (1972) *Ways of Seeing*. Penguin, London.

Bingham, K. (2023) *Exploring the Natural Underground: A New Sociology of Caving*. Routledge, Oxon.

Colley, A. (2016) *Victorians in the Mountains: Sinking the Sublime*. Routledge, Oxon.

Ekirch, R. (2005) *At Day's Close: Night in Times Past.* Norton & Company, London.

Freud, S. (1923/1961) The ego and the id. In: Strachey, J. (ed.) *The Standard Edition of the Complete Psychological Works of Sigmund Freud.* Hogarth Press, London, pp. 12–66.

Hobbes, T. (1678) *De Mirabilibus Pecci: Being the Wonders of the Peak in Darbyshire.* William Crook, London.

Hull, J. (2017) *Notes on Blindness: A Journey Through the Dark.* Profile Books, London.

Raymo, C. (2008) Why the night sky is dark. In: Bogard, P. (ed.) *Let There Be Night: Testimony on Behalf of the Dark.* University of Nevada Press, Nevada, pp. 52–60.

Sheehy, M. (2019) The Dharma of the Perfect Eon: Dolpopa Sherab Gyaltsen's Hermeneutics of Time and the Jonang Doxography of Zhentong Madhyamaka. In: Sheehy, M. and Mathes, K.-D. (eds) *The Other Emptiness: Rethinking the Zhentong Buddhist Discourse in Tibet.* Suny Press, New York, pp. 65–94.

Turner, V. (1973) The center out there: Pilgrim's goal. *History of Religions* 12(3), 191–230. DOI: 10.1086/462677.

Debilitation

8

Ouvrage Latiremont. Photo © K.P. Bingham

With the threat of Fascism growing in Europe following the First World War, long before the rise of Hitler's Third Reich in the 1930s, French military leaders became increasingly concerned about the security of their borders. Having suffered catastrophic losses against the Central Powers, it was decided that a defensive position would be more advantageous. Mindful that the machinery of war can quickly become obsolete during times of conflict, as was the case in World War One, military and political leaders concluded it would be better to delay advances into French territory while the army mobilised and new instruments of war were fast-tracked into production. Construction of a new type of fort known as 'ouvrages' ("works") therefore began in 1929 and ended in 1939. Together, the line of fortresses, underground bunkers, minefields and gun batteries became known as the 280-mile-long *Maginot Line*. Using 1.5 million cubic metres of concrete and 150,000 tons of steel, much of the fortification was buried deep in the earth. Designed to be impenetrable against heavy artillery fire and toxic gas, the largest fortifications were known as 'gros ouvrages'.

The summer of 2017 was the first time I set eyes upon a section of the Maginot Line. Some of the urban exploration crew, WildBoyz, and I had driven south of Belgium to the communes of Ugny and Baslieux to reach the Latiremont Work, one of the marvels of the line that lies at an average depth of 30 metres and consists of 1,200 metres of underground tunnels and galleries. It was a hot day and the sun shone brilliantly beneath a clear sky as we made our way to a small grove of trees that perfectly conceals one of the old gun batteries. This entrance was blocked, so our walk continued eastwards into a larger patch of woodland. We came across an observation cupola first, but true to its design it was impenetrable. Moving deeper into the trees we reached combat 'Bloc 6' next, a dreary-looking artillery block that once housed three 75mm gun embrasures and two GFM cloches. Here, one of the metal panels covering a gun portal had been partially forced open which meant there was just enough space for a person to crawl through.

Inside, the air was cold and thickly clotted with petrichor. To better perceive my surroundings, I guided my torch around a damp gallery. The torchlight illuminated bare walls the colour of cloud-filled sky, and old metal railings set in the floor that would have been used to move guns and ammunition. A tunnel leading away on the far side of the room led to the rusted cages of an old lift and a dingy staircase to the right.

Perfect for symbolism and metaphor, and more than a means of moving between points A and B, staircases have long been used to invoke feelings of smallness in observers and represent journeys of connectivity with something higher. Universally, stairs have been viewed as an analogy for freedom and spiritual ascent by means of virtue where it is possible to rise from earth into heaven, or as a means of moving towards reward of some description. As Cleo Baldon and Ib Melchior (1989) explain in their book devoted to the importance and implications of steps and their surroundings, this is why stairs are referred to as flights; with each step, they allow earthbound figures to rise to the height of birds and ethereal mist. They can, however, also have a darker side and obfuscate more than they enlighten. To move down into the dark is to enter less appealing realities and realms of the mind. It is here, to borrow Friedrich Nietzsche (1886/2003) warning about gazing into the abyss for too long, that wanderers should take care not to let the abyss also gaze into them. In the Platonic sense, what descenders have in their heads are forms. Like the shadows described in Plato's cave allegory, dwellers of darkness see only appearances and reproductions of forms and ideas rather than the real world that exists in a brighter and truer light on the surface.

Paying little attention to inner warnings, WildBoyz and I followed the stairs into the gloom. The air grew colder as we moved deeper into the fortress. After every fifty or sixty steps we seemed to reach new levels, each one unveiling more rooms and corridors to explore, but we continued to the very bottom. Having descended thousands of stairs and multiple floors, or so it felt, we emerged inside a tunnel that continued into darkness on the left but forked in two directions on the right. For the next few hours 'the Boyz' and I remained busy exploring this floor, continuing until the cold became a little too uncomfortable. Following a short discussion in the fortress's main lavatory block about whether we should stay, the group decided it was time to return to the surface. Not yet ready to leave as I was still feasting on the magic of discovery, I convinced the others it would be a good idea if I stayed a little while longer to take more photographs. Chilly and eager to feel the frisson of joy sunlight carries when it touches the skin they agreed with me, and before I could have second thoughts they were gone. Other than an occasional drip somewhere in the distance, I was suddenly alone in the darkness.

Walking with a sense of newfound freedom gave me heightened feelings of clarity. At first, I thought about Ouvrage Latiremont as quintessential modernist space. I could see how the concrete space around me represented the perfect marriage of utility and symbolism. With a central line extending north-north-east and several neatly arranged branches spread horizontally, a map of the bunker would have you think it is designed to be visually simple and easily navigable. As with Harry Beck's map of the London Underground (see: Transport for London, n.d.), the most enduring and triumphant example of angular representation that fulfils the requirements of necessary segmentation of space dreamed of by twentieth century modernists, Latiremont's layout sits tidily within the space of a discreet rectangle. The entire system, according to the map, is conceived as if it exists on one level, and that its six bunkers are the only chambers.

In many ways, I thought, Latiremont seemed to be the archetypal symbol for a new level of order sought in the period between the two world wars. Instead of conceiving the future in terms of the past, an irrational past better thought of as forgotten, developers in this era viewed concrete urban spaces as ideal for having nothing of the past in them. In other words, the utopian could be expressed by breaking completely from surface pasts, but also underground pasts associated with dirt, disease and decay, infestation and poverty, and mythical underworlds featuring diabolical scenes of fire and chaos. Reimagined in this light, the world below becomes a fantasy of total order and mechanization far removed from the contingencies of humanity.

Sadly, my thoughts about perfectly ordered underworld futures were short-lived. After just ten minutes walking alone, I entered a subterranean nightmare. Latiremont was revealing itself to be an intricate architectural labyrinth that could change, in my mind at least, at the drop of a hat. Lost was all sense of utopian potential as I had allowed it to ooze into dystopian realism. The new level of abstraction and placelessness sought by modernist architects was certainly still present, but it was the confusion of abstraction and place-lessness I was experiencing. Instead of appearing as a fixed space, Latiremont seemed to me a series of thresholds that read like a forecast of the all-too-real disorientations of modernism. This world was one of veils of darkness, unsympathetic shadows and eerie stillness. With a sense of growing frustration and the horrible sensation of not knowing north from south, I found myself in the dark, headed down unfamiliar passageways further into the unknown.

Eventually, I came into a circular chamber which seemed familiar, although I could not recall when I had encountered it before. Inside there was a vertical ladder, the second I had found since losing sight of the others, and this one led upwards to another level rather than down. Hoping with unrealistic optimism it might lead into a gun turret on the surface, I ascended. At the top, however, I quickly came to realise that it merely led into a tall assembly of rusted machinery. I was simultaneously perplexed and crushed by the intricacy of the bunker. It had not occurred to me at any other moment that it might be possible to also lose my way in structures buried within the larger structure I had slowly been exploring.

Leaving the machinery behind, I turned right to enter a long dark tunnel. I followed it hoping to find a left-hand turn. In that moment I was convinced I had originally emerged from a staircase on the left. At the first opportunity, I turned left, and then right, and then left again as I weaved my way through the confusing fortress. Water splashed over my boots as I crossed through a flooded section. The splashes echoed loudly against the cracked and pitted concrete walls. Looking out for signs of anything that seemed familiar, I walked until I eventually reached a dead end. By this point I was completely lost and cast into panic. I had no idea how far I had walked, nor a bearing on where I was relative to any previous point. In fact, I had such a sense of disorientation the panic felt primal.

As is the case in the mythological story of the Minotaur incarcerated within the ruins of the Labyrinth of Knossos, I had entered a place built to disseminate uncertainty. Latiremont was of course designed to be a space of order, but what I was discovering instead was the absurdity of rationality and within it a realm of paradox and chaos. Therein lurks the Minotaur, the creature symbolising our deepest fears and animalistic desires. Its savage cry reminded me of my impending mortality and my inherent fear of death, triggering deterioration of my normal character. I had certainly experienced disorientation before, losing my way in the North Yorkshire Moors and while roaming New Zealand's wilderness areas, but the ultimate arena of lostness I was discovering is the world of the underground. As Will Hunt (2019) explains in a chapter describing his experience of losing his bearings in the Paris catacombs, to become lost in the underground is its own species of disorientation. In the absence of subtle cues of orientation such as stars, wind direction or even the horizon, the underground becomes either blank or space composed of a language that is indecipherable.

Doing my best to maintain composure and some sense of outward calm, I backtracked until I was again in the long tunnel which I assumed was the main passage connecting each of the six main bunkers together. To my knowledge, the only way out was through the gun battery we had discovered in the forest so trying to retrace my steps seemed imperative. My plan was to move back through the rooms and tunnels systematically. I would, I decided, explore every possible inch of Latiremont until I found the familiar staircase next to the colossal lift shaft.

Retracing my steps proved to be a gruelling process. I grew increasingly frustrated as every passageway and chamber seemed to resemble every other. The same characterless concrete adorned every so often with pipes and nondescript metalwork continued no matter where I walked. As the minutes passed, I began to wonder whether the others might have started searching for me. Down one tunnel, I thought I heard someone, shuffling footsteps perhaps and whispered conversation, but when I called out nobody answered. Afterwards, I puzzled over what would happen if they too were lost. In my mind, I began to make unsettling predictions for the future. If we were all lost, there would be no one to raise the alarm. We would quickly run out of battery power in our headtorches as well, even starve to death since we had no food. Realising I only had the one light myself, I decided to adjust its setting to moonlight mode, the lowest setting available that can run continuously for fifty-days (so the manufacturer claims). The glow it cast was dim, so it slowed my progress considerably.

As the world slowed and simultaneously grew larger, it suddenly occurred to me how Xavier De Maistre (1794/2004) was able to embark on a forty-two-day long journey around his room. As he explicates, when moving through the room he rarely heads in a straight line, and when he sets off, despite having every intention of reaching a particular destination, he welcomes unhurried detours and subtle deviations: an armchair, for example, or a picture hanging in the corner. Every feature of the room, we are told, has a story to tell, from the bed curtains in the summertime when rays of sunshine disport themselves in the fabric to the bed itself which awakens more ideas than any other piece of furniture.

Having wandered tentatively into what looked like a decaying workshop, I set my gaze upon a set of drooping shelves. On them rested assorted objects. Although most were heavily corroded and indiscernible, each one could convey complex meanings and ideas. In the same way Charles Baudelaire (1867/1998) could find beauty emerging from a decomposing animal, there was something splendorous blossoming from the corruption. Elsewhere in the room I glimpsed cabinets whose contents had been ransacked and left strewn across the floor. My attention then shifted, just as it sometimes can when I read a book, to other ideas. With the shelves suddenly forgotten, my imagination pounced onto other matter and became lost among the clutter.

My intimacy with the workshop notwithstanding, as a whole I was unable to perceive the structure of the bunker. Instead, it unfolded in real time as I moved along its dark corridors. My only point of fixity was the world of the imperceptible labyrinth whose rules I was now forced to live by. It then occurred to me that labyrinths, as ancient symbols and providers of experience of prayer, healing and renewal, are intended to be tools of moral (trans)formation. As Rebecca Solnit (2014) explains, the centre of the circle or square becomes the single goal, and this allows a traveller to become absorbed in their journey. The very first length of the path, according to the traditional design, leads away from the entrance and almost reaches the centre of the labyrinth before snaking away. Only after turning their back on the end does a wanderer eventually succeed in reaching it, often when they feel the furthest away from the destination. My labyrinth, therefore, was not a labyrinth at all. Although it was modernist in design, taking its cue from practicality and usefulness and therefore a space of order, it did not represent a journey of enlightenment, salvation or initiation, or death and rebirth. What I had entered seemed more maze-like.

As an aristocratic innovation popularised in the late eighteenth century, a maze is different to a labyrinth. By design, a maze is built to confuse with its many branches and dead ends. Removing every sense of clear direction, a maze offers the confusions of free will rather than a single route to salvation. Since I had only managed to walk the wrong way, Latiremont felt unconditionally maze-like. Then again, the problem with this depiction is that Latiremont was never designed to be confounding and boundless. It was planned carefully by the Commission d'Organisation des Régions Fortifiées (CORF) and so there is absolute certainty its 'code' can be broken. This maze was therefore not a literal structure but something better resembling the ridges and convoluted folds of my mind. That is to say, the real maze was my imagination and its ability to spin thread, build structures and tell stories.

In the same way Jorge Borges (1964/2000) suggests literature is a labyrinth, and that every library contains the possibility of infinite existences and landscapes, Latiremont had become a dream-like world. Every possible turn I could make inside the bunker was a product of the winding shapes of my own imagination and it was leading me through myriad possibilities of disorientation. The way back did not exist because it was already forgotten. And with its key features misinterpreted, the way forward was a constant riddle. No matter where I walked, my efforts all seemed meaningless because I never emerged where I wanted to be. Infused, as they are in the etchings of Giovanni Piranesi's (1745-61/2010) imaginary labyrinthine prisons, were conventional scenes of known structure, together with ideal reconstructions exaggerated in scale and manipulated by multiple vanishing points. Steadily, I began to lose hope. Even if I was to somehow able see the bunker from a bird's eye perspective, I was convinced there would be no pattern or reason to my route.

What was most frustrating was that I was not lost. I knew precisely where I was and what I needed to find to get out. I was simply bewildered and there is an important distinction to be made between both conditions of being. All forms of exploring entail being lost because the explorer has never been there before and, equally, the explorer expects to become lost. I was, therefore, not an explorer in the true sense of the word. I may not have visited Latiremont before but having studied myriad pictures of the bunker and several maps beforehand I had a good idea of its layout and key features. I knew, for example, there was an ammunition depot, a narrow-gauge railway and a block containing living quarters. What is more, I knew roughly where they all were. My imagination, though, distorted things. In the same way children have little difficultly inventing fairy tales or bringing their toys and animals to life, the underground bunker had sprung free of its plans. It was now something to be investigated and travelled through but not mapped. It had become vast and intricate, an infinite interior where it was possible to keep on wandering *ad infinitum*.

With a crippling sense of helplessness, I entered yet another room that seemed alien. Logically, I must have been here before. I seemed to recall already having seen the neatly arranged fuse boxes fitted to the left-hand wall, but the peeling paint was new and unfamiliar. Everything in this room, from the metalwork to the bare concrete walls, had been painted at some point in history but after years of abandonment flakes dangled like the bark of an expanding birch. Unhappily, I sighed. I suddenly felt so discouraged it seemed burdensome to continue moving. This was not an unexpected feeling, it had been developing gradually, but now I felt the full gloom of pessimism. Overwhelmed by my inability to think clearly, I resigned myself to a condition of debilitation.

References

Baldon, C. and Melchior, I. (1989) *Steps and Stairways*. Rizzoli, New York.

Baudelaire, C. (1867/1998) *The Flowers of Evil*. Trans. J. McGowan. Oxford University Press, Oxford.

Borges, J. (1964/2000) *Labyrinths: Selected Stories and Other Writings*. Penguin, London.

De Maistre, X. (1794/2004) *A Journey around My Room and A Nocturnal Expedition around My Room*. Trans. A. Brown. Alma Books, Surry.

Hunt, W. (2019) *Underground: A Human History of the Worlds Beneath Our Feet*. Simon & Schuster, London.

Nietzsche, F. (1886/2003) *Beyond Good and Evil: Prelude to a Philosophy of the Future*. Trans. R. J. Hollingdale. Penguin, London.

Piranesi, B.G. (1745-61/2010) *The Prisons: Le Carceri*. Dover Publications.

Solnit, R. (2014) *Wanderlust: A History of Walking*. Granta, London.

Transport for London (n.d.) Harry Beck's Tube Map. [Online]. Available at: https://tfl.gov.uk/corporate/about-tfl/culture-and-heritage/art-and-design/harry-becks-tube-map

Deconstruction

9

Kaiwharawhara Cemetery (Beneath). Photo © K.P. Bingham

In the 1600s the renowned chemist Johann Becher (1669/2018) described decomposition of the human body as continual internal movement liberated from the shackles holding it in place. Arising from this mobility are the fetid, penetrating odours of the rotting corpse. While earthy parts tend to remain, everything aqueous becomes volatile and is freed in the form of pus, sanies and purge fluid. The body's cement changes rapidly and unpredictably as its components enter into other combinations that are oily and moderately saline. If accidently inhaled, the fluids emanating from a festering vessel could, Becher suggested, triumph in breaking the equilibrium of another living being's internal forces. The best course of action is to contain the leakage of miasma or, in instances where it has already escaped, avoid at all costs putrid exhalations which will likely hasten the advance of putrefaction in healthy flesh.

The smell of death lingering in the air had me worried. Somewhere between sickeningly sweet and foul, it was an odour that was stale and nauseating. Not medically trained in any way, other than having completed a first aid course, I had Becher's theory on my mind. Inhaling air loaded with noxious vapour was surely a bad idea. I was in the Kaiwharawhara stream that passes through the northwestern part of New Zealand's capital city. Although the watercourse retains most of its natural lowland sections as it flows through pastures, scrubland and native bush, some sections have been extensively modified or diverted since the late 1800s. As the city expanded, parts of the Kaiwharawhara Gulley were filled in and the stream was culverted to allow for building work on the surface. Today, 1.5 kilometres of the stream is culverted allowing it to pass beneath areas of public parkland, a former landfill site and the country's second largest cemetery.

Behind foliage that gracefully cascaded downward until it met the stream, the entrance to the culvert, a grey reinforced concrete pipe, was characterless. Once inside, I became more aware of the noise of rushing water which was magnified by the enclosed space. The stream was shallow, only two or three inches deep, but the sound gave the impression it was livelier. At first, the stream carried the enticing scent of nature: a blend of damp mosses mixed with the earthy fragrance of rich soil. The pleasant smell continued until I reached an old Second World War air-raid shelter. The shelter which still had some of its original lightbulbs *in situ* had become part of the Kaiwharawhara after the war when the watercourse was redirected to improve flood protection. It was as I neared the end of the trail of lightbulbs I noticed the smell change. Ahead, where there was perhaps once a staircase, I found a chute that would drop me into a different section of the culvert. It was here, as the aromas of the dark recesses of the earth began to stir, the air became dank and uninviting.

I had not anticipated the culvert would be contaminated by a foulness. I had decided to explore it after learning there was a population of glowworms inside. Described by William Wordsworth (1881) as 'earth born stars', and Andrew Marvell (1652/2007) as dazzling 'county comets' set against the darkness of fields, it sounded like glowworms were enchanting creatures well worth glimpsing. Glowworms have certainly inspired countless fairytales, and the poetry that hangs around them is endless. What appealed to my imagination the most is the fundamental contradiction of the glowworm which is dull by day but other-worldly by night. Although he talks about their winged cousins the firefly, Eugene Lee-Hamilton (1894) encourages us to think about the unprepossessing exterior of the creature which appears, somewhat paradoxically, to shelter the souls of those who have long been dead. In them, he suggests, is the presence of magic and the idea of afterlife.

At the bottom of the chute, I stepped into an odious passageway that was more cave-like and natural-looking than it was artificial. The walls and ceiling were of black rock that jutted out at all angles. This part of the culvert had clearly been blasted and mined by human hands, but it seemed likely that some of it was natural. Above I could see cracks virtually everywhere, some as thin as hair and others wide enough to jam my arms inside. I was aware before venturing underground that the Wellington-Hutt Valley section of the Wellington Fault, a curving 75-kilometre active seismic fault line, follows the course of the Kaiwharawhara almost perfectly. I knew, therefore, that the ground above me was likely to be riddled with more fractures and gaps than I could see. It was this that got me thinking.

In his seminal book on the history of odour, Alain Corbin (1986) talks about the ravages caused by secretions of waterlogged earth. A widely held belief in the nineteenth century was that saturated subterranean soil exudes gas unfit for respiration which later causes intermittent fever and illness. This belief engendered an obsession with fissures and faults as these were the points of contact that allowed mephitic air to percolate. The most terrible cracks were thought to be those formed by earthquakes where the earth not only spewed noxious air but absorbed and stored products of putrefaction. These cracks, it was feared, were a repository for foul substances such as faeces and corpses that would someday send the morbific fog back. The vapour, should it escape, would almost certainly corrupt or disequilibrate all living organisms. With my rational self rapidly diminishing and the smell worsening, these fears weighed heavily on my imagination. Since the source of the foul-smelling odour was entirely unknown, old beliefs about the corrupt nature of the earth became more and more conceivable. A silent fermentation threatened to engulf me. I was certain of it.

Figuring the exit was now nearer than the entrance, I edged deeper into the cave, continuing until the passage widened and the black rock started to exhibit a brown hue. Concrete had been used to line the walls on either side, presumably to reinforce the stone and keep the water contained. Here the cracks overhead seemed innumerable. Some were empty, others oozed chocolate-brown liquid, and the rest were filled with a hard silver substance that seemed inconsistent with the other colours I was seeing. Several stalactites hung from the ceiling. These formations were dark in colour, ranging from honey browns to burnt umber and even black. In caves stalactites are usually white, but these had gained colour from organic compounds leached from the soil above. As I continued walking, the stalactites grew larger and more numerous and the foul odour gained intensity. It suddenly dawned on me that I was, almost certainly, now directly beneath the cemetery.

In his book on the aesthetics of ugliness, Karl Rosenkranz (1853/2015) suggests it would be a terrifyingly disgusting picture if we were to take a city such as Paris and turn it upside down. With the bottommost part of the city on top, a hideous amalgam of decay, sludge and light-avoiding creatures would all of a sudden be visible to the eye. The runoffs from the gutters, rags and other remnants of human culture, and animals that thrive on decay would appear with the same majestic theatre of a fire-spitting mountain. Incredibly, I was bearing witness to this absurd upside-down world. This was a world not of the wilting and dying, but rather the decomposition of the already dead. My senses were fired, outraged with disgust knowing products of nature, from excrement and slime to sweat and abscesses, were thickly crusted to the walls. I withered away from the long finger-like stalactites stretching low enough to sweep my head. Having clawed their way through dirt and rock, the raw tipped fingers now trickled into the open. As they dripped down from the ceiling, they sealed the fissures and coated everything beneath their path with a brownish glaze.

The walls themselves, having entered the vicious cycle of decay, wept with every symptom of 'concrete cancer'. Deep inside the human-made material, deleterious swelling was causing extensive cracking and flaking. Where bolts had been drilled to support pipework, they had swollen with rust and eroded into brittle flakes. Close to me on the left, there was a different section whose face appeared to have melted as it now wore the hardened flesh of bodily juices. This substance was smooth and white yet bore the scars of unevenly spread boils that looked pus-filled, tender and ready to rupture.

As I stooped lower to avoid a particularly long stalactite, the stream caught my attention. It was moving steadily which is normally a sign the current has dissolved and expelled all objects of putrefaction lodged in the water particles. What I saw, however, was water stirred up with sinister bubblings as it was overloaded with disturbed silt and other substances that were foreign to it. It was filled with worms, rotten vegetation and dead insects and, like the air I was breathing, tainted by a great deal of yellowish material. More like the oily, bone-filled River Styx than a natural stream, it seemed perilous to lay my bare hands in it. Later, though, this was unavoidable when I stumbled and had a split-second to choose whether to fall into the sickeningly crusted wall or the decomposition circulating in the stream. Afterwards, as I dried my hands on my jacket, I was convinced I could feel my skin rupture as the rot set in. Just like the character Mary in Ian Rankin's (1986) novel *The Flood* who is pushed into a chemical-filled burn, I had strayed into a place I did not belong. As Rankin describes it, this was a warm dying place.

Our common experience of decay and morbidity is one of avoidance mostly. Death and decay await us all, people and objects alike, yet this thought is a nauseating one. It is therefore unsurprising, as Caitlin DeSilvey (2017) writes, that conservation, sanitisation and sterilization are common coping mechanisms in our day-to-day lives. Indeed, I would have given anything to have had the protection of any one of these strategies while walking the Kaiwharawhara stream. I am used to people showing signs of aging and, like every other human, have the ability to discard and dispose of the things that have reached the end of their life cycle. What I am less familiar with are the physical process and the changes that occur following deterioration and death. Even in my exploration of several abandoned mortuaries some years earlier, I had not faced decay, dirt and disease so intimately. The task of purifying it had been given to science, and its steel benches, white tiles and embalming tables were still doing their job of keeping death in check.

As I fretted about touching the stream water, it occurred to me that decay may be a token of the human condition but taboo because in being neither alive nor sufficiently dead it threatens the borders of the living. It was chilling to think about but as they slowly seeped into the Kaiwharawhara the fragmented, mutilated and unrecognisable bodies of the past brought to me the vivid reality of life and death and its unending struggle with time. In many ways, the stalactites were like the remains of lit candles in that they were yellowed, waxy and nearly spent. Consumed by an earth that refused to sustain them, these beings may have been skeletally dead but still oozing and flowing they retained faint traces of life. In the everyday world, cultural ceremonies, rituals and laws of prohibition serve to prevent people from coming into contact with scenes of such defilement, but as there were no ceremonies, rituals and laws in the world I had entered the grotesque chorography could play out without much hinderance.

It was, I think, the general sliminess of my surroundings that repulsed me the most. Slime is neither solid nor liquid but something in between and it moves in slow motion. It is an aberrant substance that gives the feeling it might absorb everything in its path, and that we will not be able to rid ourselves of it should it be touched. As Jean-Paul Sartre (1943/2018) suggests in *Being and Nothingness*, only at the moment we believe we possess it does it become clear it possesses us. Hence, I was appalled when I noticed slime on my trouser leg. On impulse I scrubbed it, hoping it would somehow disappear, but the more I tried to remove the stain the more it smeared like bacon fat. In the end it leached through the fabric and was spread so widely I could feel, smell and almost taste it.

As I neared the end of the stalactites and the structure of the culvert became bunker-like once again, I noticed something in the water up ahead. Half-submerged in the yellow murk, a blob of smooth grey matter. As I drew closer, I realised it was a large eel and judging by the smell it had been there for some time; the stench of its oils, fats and mottled flesh had spread wildly through the entire passage. Its head, mouldy and collapsed and covered in grey-white fur, was now unrecognisable. With the irrational part of me fearing it would suddenly spring to life and surge in my direction, I stepped tentatively around the wretched creature. Once I was clear, I instinctively trotted for a few steps to increase the distance between us. As I walked, I could not help but feel the rotten eel was slithering behind me, leaving in its wake a sticky yellow-brown trail. A cold shiver ran down my spine.

There was a corner up ahead, twisting left into darkness. In that direction, I could sense the air was different. Already I could detect a combination of earthy, woody and herbal aromas, intermingling to create a rich fragrance that was crisper and clean. The clammy moisture inside the culvert seemed to make the smell more penetrating than it would be outside, and denser with sensory information. I glanced back and for a moment imagined the contents of the underworld leaving with me. Like the apple that was forgotten soon after it was bitten, whose fruit-flesh shrivelled and blackened and spread rot, disease and parasites throughout the Garden of Eden, the passageway seemed ready to breathe on the outside world with its rotten breath. With decay clinging to my clothes, skin and hair, I contemplated whether I might have become the fruit. The danger, as Jenny Hval (2018) writes, is that the apple has no end as all of Eden followed its example and from that moment on started to decompose.

I would later ponder that even the glowworms I had seen were as much a part of the deconstruction of the living as everything else I had witnessed inside the culvert. As I was to discover, the shimmering larvae actually belonged to fungus gnats, a species of gnat endemic to Australia and New Zealand that carries mushroom spores and parasitic diseases such as pythium. If such creatures do enshrine the spirits of the dead, I thought, they do so as swarms that aid in the decomposition of organic matter. As hazy clouds of seemingly uncoordinated movement that often choose to crawl rather than fly and can tolerate freezing temperatures due to their possession of antifreeze proteins, it seemed more plausible they were servants of Beezlebub than creatures of enchantment. Servants to the withered but powerful 'Lord of the Flies' who feeds greedily on the decaying bodies of the deceased.

References

Becher, J. (1669/2018) *Physica Subterranea*. Forgotten Books, London.

Corbin, A. (1986) *The Foul and the Fragrant: Odor and the French Social Imagination*. Berg Publishers, Leamington Spa.

DeSilvey, C. (2017) *Curated Decay: Heritage Beyond Saving*. University of Minnesota Press, Minneapolis.

Hval, J. (2018) *Paradise Rot*. Trans. M. Idriss. Verso, London.

Lee-Hamilton, E. (1894) Fireflies. In: *Sonnets of the Wingless Hours*. Stone & Kimball, Chicago.

Marvell, A. Smith, N. (ed.). (1652/2007) *The Poems of Andrew Marvell*. Pearson, Harlow.

Rankin, I. (1986) *The Flood*. Speaking Volumes, Naples, Florida.

Rosenkranz, K. (1853/2015) *Aesthetics of Ugliness: A Critical Edition*. Trans. A. Pop and M. Widrich. Bloomsbury, London.

Sartre, J.-P. (1943/2018) *Being and Nothingness: An Essay in Phenomenological Ontology*. Routledge, Oxon.

Wordsworth, W. (1881) *The Poetical Works of Wordsworth*. Frederick Warne and Co, London.

Displeasure

10

The Twilight Zone. Photo © K.P. Bingham

In 1882 one of the most influential and oft-cited minds suggested that life's greatest rewards spring from encounters with adversity. This mind belonged to Friedrich Nietzsche (1882/2020), and he was convinced a meaningful existence depends upon a person's relationship with fulfilment and suffering. For Nietzsche, pleasure and displeasure are bound together so tightly whoever wants as much as possible of one must have as much as possible of the other. Everybody has a choice he explains, either to accept as little displeasure as possible or as much displeasure as possible, but it should be expected that feelings of joy are lessened the more desire there is to diminish and lower levels of pain and suffering.

I do not believe Nietzsche was speaking nihilistically. Although he was greatly influenced by Arthur Schopenhauer, the German philosopher who has been described as one of the 'founding fathers' of nihilism, what he arrived at was the conviction that hardship is the catalyst for happiness and fulfilment. Nietzsche's point, contrary to Schopenhauer's counsel that the wise should devote their lives to avoiding pain, is that unhappiness and unfulfillment are both natural and inevitable on the way to reaching anything good. Embracing it is therefore essential because it makes a person better for it. To articulate the idea more clearly, Nietzsche uses the metaphor of the strongest tree:

> Examine the lives of the best and the most fruitful people and peoples and ask yourselves whether a tree that is supposed to grow to a proud height can dispense with bad weather and storms; whether misfortune and external resistance, some kinds of hatred, jealousy, stubbornness, mistrust, hardness, avarice, and violence do not belong among the *favourable* conditions without which any great growth even of virtue is scarcely possible.

It might appear that the notes contained in this book support Nietzsche's idea of suffering as a necessary ingredient of fulfilment. However, as much as I agree there is pleasure to be found in displeasure, this has not been my focus. What I have attempted to unpack instead is a condition of astonishment and wonder that occurs during an unpleasurable liminal moment. Just as Karl Rosenkranz (1853/2015) challenges the preconception that no good art could be ugly, my intention has been to show that it may be an achievement to acknowledge the endless multiplicity of disorganisations of displeasure. In my own way and through the medium of walking dangerously, it is the cosmos of displeasure and the disagreeable I have revealed, from its minor twinges to its most intense formations of chaos, incorrectness and destruction.

To value displeasure in and of itself is to challenge the unequal nature of binary oppositions. As Jacques Derrida (1973) famous argued, meaning in day-to-day life is often defined in terms of binary oppositions and usually one side of each binary pair is preferred over the other. Good, for example, is normally favoured over evil. Challenging binary oppositions is important, Derrida suggests, because couplets are far from natural; in the way they are set up, there is always a degree of arbitrariness to them. In terms of walking, its roots tend to be in pleasure, happiness and enjoyment which means displeasure, unhappiness and boredom are naturally its antithesis. To view walking in such a positive way is to assume it has a true essence and agree that anything other than joy must be cast aside in order to maintain its purity. I have, for this reason, intentionally deconstructed this idea and in the process undermined the prevailing judgement that walking should not be unpleasant.

Given the focus of the book, there were times I found it challenging to write. There is no denying that seeking out pleasure is endlessly more satisfying than trying to immerse oneself in displeasure so there were many instances while I was writing I wanted to be thinking about something else. It is natural, I believe, that we associate creativity with joy since it is a clear catalyst for motivation and an inner stimulus towards action, and I can see why it is preferable to write in the service of pleasure. What urged me to continue nonetheless was the thought that we cannot always avoid or ignore displeasure. Just as epidemiologists must examine a disease intimately before they ever discover a cure, from the many discolourations and disfigurations it causes in all its swollen, ulcerated, emaciated and pallid forms to the inevitable destruction it can bring about, my thinking was that scholars and writers of walking should follow suit and embrace unpleasantness more often. I feel that representing the origins of displeasure, along with its various modes and its possibilities, in relation to walking especially, has interesting creative potential.

In the case of this book, displeasure is explored through the conceptual lens of liminality because when a person walks dangerously they find themselves bound to a particular situation that is *in-between*. Ambiguity, as Siegfried Kracauer (1969) explains, is an unavoidable part of this inbetweenness and whoever is located in such space can become attuned to the presence of adverse or conflicting possibilities. The liminal cannot always be adequately represented but exploratory efforts can help give form to threshold realities by making some of their contours visible. Much of this book is a theatre of memory and taken together its chapters can be viewed as an attempt to unpack those contours, unveiling intimately, intuitively and empathetically experiences of the betwixt and between.

In Chapter 3 desolation in the North Yorkshire Moors was explored to break down romantic perceptions of moorland where the landscape is viewed as an endless tapestry of rich tones and yellow hues when sunshine brightens the grasses. Without the distraction of beautiful colour, my attention turned to the incomprehensible enormity of landscape, the decaying deposits of matter that lie beneath the peat and mire, and feelings of separation that seemed unshakable at the time. Any guidebook describing the moors will usually tell its readers about the charm of broad expanse and the glorious medley of colour when heather is in bloom, but these are sights that can be taken in from the fringes of the moorland proper. What a guidebook will generally not reveal is the grand desolation of the interior.

When the roads and footpaths disappear, a tract of lonely country is entered that is more studded with illusory trails, immemorial remains and shattered monuments than most other places. This is a forgotten region of a primal world, a wasteland of endless rot and decay where strong winds, or sometimes no wind at all, carry sounds that are not normally heard. The moor is not always desolate, but when it is its waters settle as black and treacherous bog and its grasses whisper with solitary tone. Prying figures seem to hide in the rugged turfy landscape, ill-wishing people as they attempt to lure them into desolate solitude. The loneliness of the moorland can be charming, but it can become terrible and oppressive if a person's mood loses its buoyancy. In places like the North Yorkshire Moors, even the strongest minds can surrender to superstition. From barghests to bottomless pools haunted by death and tragedy, the moors are neither real nor imaginary. Like Brocéliande, the enchanted forest that had a reputation in medieval European imagination as a place of magic and mystery, the moors can too easily follow the logic of myth, dream and nightmare.

In Chapter 4, my focus shifted to discontentment in the Lake District. What I wanted to demonstrate is that discontents can arise from the freedom of pleasure-seeking which tolerates too little security. Often, when we carry in our minds an image of adventure, we visualise how it will kindle enthusiasm and make every nerve end quiver in awe. Nature's peace, we are told by John Muir (1894), will flow into you when you climb a mountain, just as sunshine pours into trees. Yet, there are moments when adventure does not deliver in the way we might have expected.

Walking through fog, or deluges so intense you could part the water like a curtain, makes navigation very difficult if not nearly impossible. Suddenly, after having made judgement from a map, the terrain no longer matches what you were expecting and discontentment sets in. As you shelter from the worst of the weather, perhaps in a bivvy or a shallow crack in a rock, confusion, fear and cold compete for equal time. With the body's resources reaching the point of depletion, strength seems like it is utterly diminished. It is the cold, in particular, that casts a potent spell, one capable of dragging you into a deepened state of misery. It comes as no surprise to think that freezing wildernesses, deserts and mountains alike were long regarded as worthless and forbidding places before they were ever beautiful. On the wrong day, when they appear as extreme terrains of danger and disaster, they are ugly and incommodious. What is worse still is that when you finally succumb to discontentment, it leads nowhere. Focus and attention are fixated solely on grievances that become intolerable. In the end, the urge to flee hurriedly becomes too great to ignore.

In Chapter 5 the focus of the theatre of memory changed from rural to urban walking as I explored the derelict remains of a boatbuilder's workshop and yard. The purpose of this chapter was to explore the dangers of 'Otherness' and becoming the 'Other'. Following several of Zygmunt Bauman's (1993) key ideas, my point is that *vagabonds* are created in a world dedicated to *tourists*. Vagabonds, as Bauman explains, are viewed as the waste of the world, delinquents and non-entities that need to be subdued because they fail to consume in the correct way. The bodies of such individuals are inescapably dirty and the language of contagion, infection and poor hygiene has frequently been used to frame them. In the case of this book, the vagabond is the trespasser who challenges the idea they exist within a bubble where space is plentiful but mostly hidden behind walls. However, stepping into space delineated by walls, fences, signs or even imaginary lines inevitably turns the inclination of the law against the trespasser. To wander or roam freely is to stray from clearly established lines of moral behaviour and the limits of acceptable action. Walking, that simplest of actions the human body has evolved to do, is therefore frequently wrapped in a moral stigma that runs deeply through the heart of civil life.

With my focus still on the urban world, Chapter 6 explores the crumbling power and downward pull of loss and ruination. Contrary to Georg Simmel's

(1859–1918/1959) view that the appearance of nature in a decaying building can invoke a profound sense of peace and utopian potential, my experience
in Christchurch Cathedral involved a different kind of contemplative gaze.
Instead of interpreting the return of a cathedral to nature as space that was
magically surreal or celebrating it as a site of reconciliation and remembrance,
I saw it as a reminder that the things we value will inevitably be erased from
the world. Processes that should have been impossible, those seen in collapsed
and broken bell towers, a missing choir room, the distorted pipes of an organ,
and in the olive-green decay of stone walls, firmly imprinted themselves in
my imagination as the penetrability of the uncanny. As an expression of total
ambiguity, the cathedral stood as an unintelligible mass of odious destruction.
Offset only occasionally by the crunch of stone or glass, here was a world
where gaunt stillness and silence had full ascendency over bustle and noise. In
the full sense of the word, a phantasmagoria of mystery and horror was found.
Having humanised the sacred, the cathedral was somehow a mockery of life,
filling it with the unavoidable terror of our mortality. As I saw it, God was dead
and even today there is something terribly disconcerting about that thought.

As the focus of the theatre of memory shifted to underground walking,
attention was turned to the destructive power of darkness and isolation in
a cave known as Sidetrack. From time to time most people experience some
desire to be alone, but when it happens unexpectedly and in total darkness
the effects of separation and visual deprivation can take a heavy toll. In
such moments, darkness can be terrifying. To have the final traces of light
sensation disappear completely and then be unable to discern day from
night or up from down is to be swallowed whole by a monster. As it strips
away rational thought and replaces it for emotion and pure sensation in the
form of smell, touch, taste and sound, darkness of this kind makes a person
vulnerable. With all visual motion suspended and the mind so entirely
filled with existential terror, comprehension of the fragility of human life is
acquired together with greater appreciation for the immeasurable vastness
of emptiness.

In many ways, what Chapter 7 reveals without directly saying so is that
experiences of darkness overlap with Levinas's (1978/2001) ontology of the
night which is based on the rejection of otherness as it appears in conditions of
light. What Levinas means is that light may be the mechanism through which
otherness appears, but it is only in darkness a person is rendered open to the
other. Light, in other words, functions as a protective barrier, a boundary separating a person from otherness which is usually held at a distance. In darkness,
the distance is broken and everything other, while still hidden and unknown,
is felt more closely and intimately. In a Deleuzo-Guattarian sense, this might
be understood as a means of constituting a body-without-organs (Deleuze
and Guattari, 1987) because darkness makes people more open towards being
affected by the world. In darkness the world is reduced, people experience
what it is like to lose touch with the certainty of their subjectivity and they
are scorched by desperation, but at the same time they enter an apparently

irremediable void where there are possibilities for new and unexpected interactions with objects and space.

My journey underground continued in Chapter 8 as I explored a disconcerting site of illusion, memory and incoherency. It was the image of a labyrinth that served loosely as a framework for better understanding this new reality because, as Victor Tschudi (2022) points out, there is nothing more devious than a labyrinthine structure with exits that leads nowhere. After entering Ouvrage Latiremont, descending its staircases, traversing its corridors and weaving my way through its endless rooms, I could conclude that I was uncertain how many staircases, corridors and rooms there were since my imagination and anxiety had multiplied them. What I generated was a structure that could have derived from one of Giovanni Piranesi's sinister prison etchings, for it seemed exaggerated in scale and unfolded according to no logical plan. As an impossible structure, Latiremont consisted of stairways that gave access to seemingly impenetrable walls, of rooms that were impossible to ever find again, and of entranceways that opened either into hulks of rusting machinery or into corridors so long I am convinced they had to have been dreamt. Stripped of its many layers of metaphor, it becomes clear that my depiction of Latiremont is actually a map of the mind which can obfuscate more than enlighten. Every path that could be followed was a mystery within the mysterious and this had a debilitating effect because architecture that simply goes on corresponds to a life that has lost purpose and meaning.

Drawing together in one walk the three distinct realms of walking that are explored in this book, those of the rural, the urban and the underground, Chapter 9 dispenses with everything about the everyday world that is spellbinding and enchanting. My intention with this chapter was to give the reader a detailed illustration of an alternative world that offers rich potential for a different and more conflicted kind of existence. The image presented of the culverted Kaiwharawhara stream, which contains everything unworthy of dwelling in the present from contents of past to the rejected and the condemned, is one of raw ambivalence, fragmentation and obsolescence. Far from imprisoning its visitors in their own subjectivity this world opens up ignored, unseen and often warped seams of thought, teaching us about the connections that exist between displeasure and the creative potentials of the imagination. Of the book as a whole but Chapter 9 especially, it might be said that walking dangerously is an important deconstructive endeavour as it helps conceive new ways of seeing. A successful deconstruction, that term derived from the work of Jacques Derrida (1976), stimulates a mode of critical inquiry that opposes taken-for-granted assumptions about walking and indeed even leisure more generally. Such an inquiry should prompt changes in our perceptions not only about the potential but the limits of enduring unpleasant liminal episodes.

Reflecting on some of the liminal experiences I have had over the years while walking dangerously has broadened and deepened my feelings for displeasure. I am no longer just a pleasure-seeker when I walk. Now, I occasionally find myself choosing to overcome desires for convenience, comfort and joy. To feel fully human and experience a richer sense of the freedom walking has to offer is to go against the usual rules of disenchantment. Rather than overcome disenchantment, my suggestion in this book is to try embracing it for what it is. As I mentioned at the beginning of the chapter, I suggest this not for reasons of joy or for pleasure sought through the enchantment of disenchantment but for the sake of valuing displeasure in and of itself. To understand walking when it is joyous and never foul is to appreciate only half its story. Witnessing moors so bleak and calamitous it is impossible to enjoy them, darkness so crushing it impels you to claw earth in a maddened frenzy, and the odious dead as they ooze and seep from their resting places is the other half. Seeing and living through such things is to be baptised into a richer and more deeply felt relationship with walking.

References

Bauman, Z. (1993) *Postmodern Ethics*. Blackwell, London.

Deleuze, G. and Guattari, F. (1987) *A Thousand Plateaus: Capitalism and Schizophrenia*. University of Minnesota Press, Minneapolis.

Derrida, J. (1973) *Speech and Phenomena, and Other Essays on Husserl's Theory of Signs*. Northwestern University Press, Evanston.

Derrida, J. (1976) *Of Grammatology*. Johns Hopkins University Press, Baltimore.

Kracauer, S. (1969) *History: The Last Things Before the Last*. Oxford University Press, Oxford.

Levinas, E. (1978/2001) *Existence and Existents*. Duquesne University Press, Pennsylvania.

Muir, J. (1894) *The Mountains of California*. The Century Co, New York.

Nietzsche, F. (1882/2020) *The Gay Science*. Dover, New York.

Rosenkranz, K. (1853/2015) *Aesthetics of Ugliness*. Trans. A. Pop and M. Widrich. Bloomsbury, London.

Simmel, G. (1859-1918/1959) The ruin. In: Wolff, K.H. (ed.) *A Collection of Essays with Translations and A Bibliography*. Ohio State University Press, Columbus, pp. 259–263.

Tschudi, V.P. (2022) *Piranesi and the Modern Age*. MIT Press, Cambridge, Massachusetts.

www.ingramcontent.com/pod-product-compliance
Lightning Source LLC
Chambersburg PA
CBHW050805270326
41926CB00025B/4555